WINDOWS FOR WORKGROUPS 3.11
in easy steps

HARSHAD KOTECHA

First published in 1994

Computer Step
Unit 5c, Southfield Road
Southam, Leamington Spa
Warwickshire CV33 OJH
United Kingdom

Tel. +44 (0)926 817999
Fax. +44 (0)926 817005

Copyright © 1994 by Harshad Kotecha

All rights reserved. No part of this book may be reproduced or transmitted in any form or by any means, electronic or mechanical, including photocopying, recording, or by any information storage or retrieval system, without prior written permission from the publisher.

Notice of Liability
Every effort has been made to ensure that this book contains accurate and current information. However, Computer Step and the author shall not be liable for any loss or damage suffered by readers as a result of any information contained herein.

Trademarks
Microsoft® and MS-DOS® are registered trademarks and Microsoft At Work, Windows™ and the Windows for Workgroups logo are trademarks of Microsoft Corporation. TrueType® is a registered trademark of Apple Computer Inc, Paintbrush™ is a trademark of ZSoft Corporation. All other trademarks are acknowledged as belonging to their respective companies.

British Library Cataloguing in Publication Data
A catalogue record for this book is available from the British Library.

Printed in England

ISBN 1 874029 12 1

Table of Contents

An Overview 1
Benefits of Windows 1
Benefits of Workgroups 2
Getting started 3
Conventions used in this book 4

1. The Basics 5
Using a Mouse 7
Starting Windows for Workgroups 8
Using Menus/Dialog Boxes 10
Moving a Window 11
Maximising/Restoring Windows 12
Minimising/Restoring Windows 13
Resizing Windows 14
Rearranging Icons 15
Arranging Icons Automatically 15
Moving between Group Windows 16
Cascading Group Windows 17
Tiling Group Windows 18
Scrolling Group Windows 19
Closing Windows 20
Using On-screen Help 21
Invoking Context-sensetive Help 24
Starting a Mouse Tutorial 24
Exiting Windows for Workgroups 25

2. Working with Applications 27
Setting up Program Groups 29
Setting up Programs 31
Setting up several Programs 33
Setting up Non-Windows Programs 35
Starting an Application 37
Working with several Programs 38
Using the Task List 39
Using the Clipboard 41

Saving the Clipboard 42
Displaying ClipBook Pages 44
Copying ClipBook Pages into the Clipboard 45
Deleting ClipBook Pages 45
Sharing ClipBook Pages 46
Unsharing ClipBook Pages 46
Connecting to a shared ClipBook 47
Disconnecting from a shared ClipBook 47
Exiting to the MS-DOS Prompt 48
Automating Startups 49
Organising your Desktop 50

3. Managing your Files 53

Starting File Manager 55
Splitting Tree/Directory Window 56
Viewing Tree/Directory 57
Viewing more Information on Files 58
Sorting Files 59
Working with Multiple Windows 60
Changing the Screen Font 61
Changing Disk Drives 62
Changing Directories 62
Expanding Directory Branches 63
Creating New Directories 64
Sharing your Directories 65
Unsharing your Directories 66
Connecting to a Shared Directory 67
Seeing who is using your Directories 69
Disconnecting from a Shared Directory 71
Selecting Files 72
Copying/Moving Files or Directories 74
Deleting Files or Directories 78
Undeleting Files or Directories 79
Renaming Files or Directories 81
Searching for Files 82
Changing File Attributes 83
Associating Files to Applications 84
Starting Applications from Files 85
Formatting a Disk 86

Labelling a Disk 87
Copying a Disk 88
Scanning for Viruses 89
Backing up your Hard Disk 90

4. Printing 91
Accessing Printers 93
Installing a Printer 94
Setting up a Printer 95
Installing Fonts 96
Printing from Applications 97
Using Drag and Drop Printing 98
Using the Print Manager 100
Controlling Printing 102
Using Separator Pages 103
Sharing your Printer 104
Unsharing your Printer 105
Connecting to a Network Printer 106
Disconnecting from a Network Printer 108

5. Customising 109
Changing the Screen Colours 111
Adding a Desktop Pattern 113
Adding a Wallpaper 114
Using Screen Savers 115
Using Fast Alt+Tab Switching 116
Changing the Icon Spacing 116
Using the Sizing Grid box 116
Changing the Cursor Blink Rate 116
Customising your Mouse 117
Changing the Keyboard Response 118
Resetting the Date/Time 119
Setting Country-specific Standards 120
Using Ports 121
Using 386 Enhanced 121
Using Sound 121
Changing Network Settings 122
Customising the File Manager Toolbar 124
Customising Help 126

6. General and Network Accessories 127

Opening the Accessories Group 129
Using Write 130
Using Paintbrush 133
Using Notepad 135
Using Clock 135
Using Cardfile 136
Using Calendar 137
Using Calculator 138
Using Terminal 139
Using Recorder 139
Using Character Map 139
Using Media Player 140
Using Sound Recorder 140
Opening the Network Group 141
Using Chat 142
Using NetWatcher 144
Using WinMeter 144
Using WinPopup 145
Logging Off 147
Logging On 147
Remote Access 147
Network Setup 148
Fax Facilities 148

7. Mail and Schedule+ 149

Setting up a Workgroup Postoffice 151
Adding a User to the Postoffice 153
Changing User Information 154
Removing a User 155
Getting into Mail 156
Sending a Message 157
Message Options 159
Reading/Replying to Mail Messages 160
Deleting Mail Messages 161
Creating New Folders 162
Moving Messages between Folders 163
Forwarding Messages 164

Exiting from Mail 164
Getting into Schedule+ 165
Adding Appointments 166
Adding Recurring Appointments 168
Using the Task List 169
Scheduling a Meeting 171
Exiting from Schedule+ 172

8. Object Linking and Embedding 173

What is OLE? 175
Linking an Object 176
Embedding an Object 177
Changing a Linked Object 178
Changing an Embedded Object 179
Using Object Packager 180

Index 181

An Overview

Workgroup computing is based on a well-known saying, "The whole is greater than the sum of its parts". This is certainly true of *Windows for Workgroups* (WFWG) - a popular networking product for small groups utilising the *Microsoft Windows* operating system.

WFWG version 3.11 is an updated version of the Windows 3.1 operating system. It can be used even if your computer is not networked with others. Obviously, networking features will then not be available, but the enhanced performance and other minor improvements still justify its use.

WFWG allows you to share resources like the printer and communicate information between your colleages effectively so that everyone in a team is more productive. Potential benefits are substantial - even in a small team of say just two people 'workgrouped'.

Many organisations have already standardised on using WFWG in their offices. What is now needed is a cost-effective way of training users to make the most of the networking capability and at the same time learning Windows, so that maximum benefits can be gained from the product.

This book aims to do just that. It combines stunning screen shots, exactly as they appear in the product, with simple, clear instructions on how to perform specific tasks - leaving out the unnecessary verbal blurb!

Benefits of Windows

The basic foundation underlying Windows is its 'windowing' capability. A window is a rectangular area used to display information or to run an application. Several windows can be opened at the same time to work with multiple applications and therefore, increasing productivity on a personal computer (PC).

Windows also uses pictures or graphical symbols (called *icons*) to represent applications and functions. This whole *Graphical User Interface* (or 'Gooey' as it is commonly known as) makes it much easier and more intuitive to work.

Software designed to run under Windows has the same consistent 'look and feel'. Therefore, once you have learned to use one Windows package, it is much easier to learn another. Examples include *Word for Windows*, *Excel for Windows* and *WordPerfect for Windows*.

Several of these programs can run at the same time under Windows. This feature is known as *Multitasking*. For example, you can start printing a large document from your word-processor and whilst that task is going-on, open another 'window' to start work on your spreadsheet.

A powerful feature, called *Object Linking and Embedding* (OLE) lets you share information (objects) by allowing you to link/embed them in new documents you create - even though the 'objects' were not created using the same application. For example, you can link or embed a graphic created using a drawing software package into a word processor document.

Using Windows, you can also organise and customise your desktop (the whole computer screen in other words) to the way you prefer to work.

Benefits of Workgroups

A workgroup is a group of computers linked together (as a *Network*) so that you can work more efficiently by:

- (a) sharing resources (like the printer)
- (b) sharing information (like a report that several people are working on)
- (c) communicating with each other easily

Several workgroups can be set up - say one for each department - or you may simply have a single workgroup in an organisation linking all its computers together. One of the main advantages of using workgroups is that there is no need to transfer information between computers using floppy disks.

To share facilities, the owner must designate them as being shared. Once this has been done, others in the workgroup will be able to have access to them. The sharing of facilities can be cancelled at any time.

Since information security may be important it is possible to restrict access to computers, files and printers by the use of passwords known only to those entitled to use these facilities. It is also possible to allow more than one person to use the same computer by allocating a separate password for each one.

A variety of communication systems also exists to allow users in a workgroup to pass information between themselves.

A *Mail* facility allows you to write messages and send them to other users in the workgroup. To run this facility, one computer in each workgroup must be set up to act as a *Postoffice* to oversee the distribution of mail.

Schedule+ allows you to organise your appointments and co-ordinate meetings and activities with other members in your workgroup.

Modems can be shared using the network, giving all users access to the *Fax* facilities in WFWG.

A further facility called *Chat* allows you to type messages directly onto the screens of up to seven other users, letting you hold an interactive conversation.

Getting started

To enable you to become part of a workgroup, your computer must be linked to another. This is done by installing a special device, called a *Network card*, in your computer. The network card controls the communication of your computer with another in the network which also has to have a network card. The computers are then physically connected (via the network cards) using special cables and connectors.

This book assumes that the installation of network cards and linking of computers has already been done and that the WFWG software has been installed on each of the computers. After this has been done, you have to give your computer a name by which it can be identified, specify a password, and assign it to a workgroup.

Conventions used in this book

1. Keys that are used in combination are represented with a '+' sign in between. For example,

    Alt+F

    The above implies that you should press and hold down the 'Alt' key, then tap the 'F' key once.

2. If you are not using a mouse follow this keyboard convention which is similar to that used in the product displays too;

    (a) where a word in the text has a letter printed in bold and underlined (for example **F**ile) press Alt+the underlined letter to access a menu, button or check box.

    (b) Simply type the underlined letter if you are choosing an option from a displayed menu (for example **N**ew...).

3. ▷ indicates that the topic continues on the next page.

4. ◁ indicates that the topic has continued from the previous page.

In this book you will learn how to take advantage of all general Windows features and also the new Workgroup features incorporated in WFWG. It has been designed so that you can read it from start to finish, go directly to chapters that are of interest, or alternatively just refer to the relevant topics within a chapter.

Good luck!

CHAPTER 1

The Basics

THIS CHAPTER COVERS

- Using a Mouse
- Starting Windows for Workgroups
- Using Menus/Dialog Boxes
- Moving a Window
- Maximising/Restoring Windows
- Minimising/Restoring Windows
- Resizing Windows
- Rearranging Icons
- Arranging Icons Automatically
- Moving between Group Windows
- Cascading Group Windows
- Tiling Group Windows
- Scrolling Group Windows
- Closing Windows
- Using On-screen Help
- Invoking Context-sensitive Help
- Starting a Mouse Tutorial
- Exiting Windows for Workgroups

in easy steps

Using a Mouse

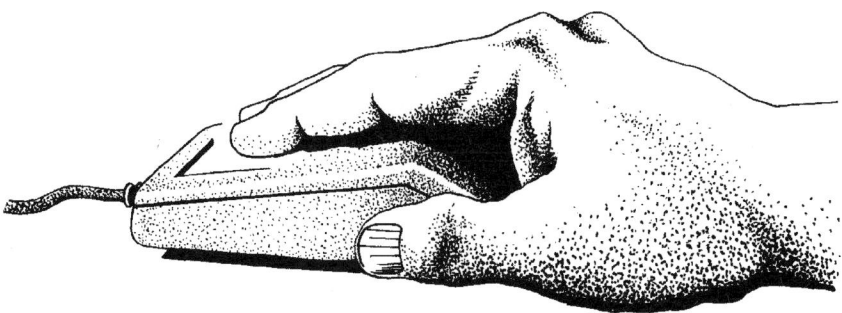

A mouse is a pointing device used to communicate with your computer. It is recommended that you use Microsoft, or Microsoft-compatible mouse with *Windows for Workgroups*.

To use it, first place it on a flat surface or use a mouse mat. You will notice an arrow-headed pointer ( ) moving on your screen as you move the mouse.

To make a selection, move the mouse pointer on top of an item and then press and release (or click) the left mouse button. Sometimes you can click twice in rapid succession to select an item (double-click).

A mouse can also be used to move items on the screen. This is achieved by first moving the mouse pointer over an item. Then, press and hold down the left mouse button and move the mouse to position the item. Finally, once you see the item in the new location, release the mouse button. This technique is called 'dragging'.

In this guide we will use the terms: Click, Double-click and Drag to refer to mouse operations described above.

Starting Windows for Workgroups

Tip
*Type **WIN** : if you do not want to see the Microsoft Windows for Workgroups logo on startup.*

It is assumed that you have *Windows for Workgroups* (WFWG) installed on your PC in a directory, WINDOWS. To start WFWG, type:

    WIN

at the DOS prompt.

Note
You may automatically get this screen after you switch on your computer if the WIN command is entered in the autoexec.bat file.

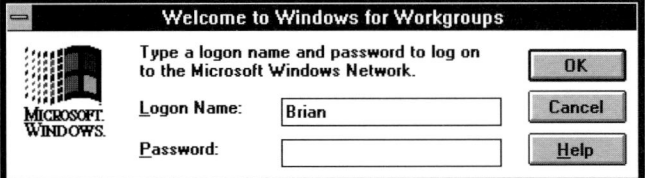

A screen called Welcome to Windows for Workgroups will be displayed, which will display your logon name. You should type your password in and press the Enter key on the keyboard or use the mouse to click on the OK button. If you are using WFWG for the first time, the following screen will be displayed.

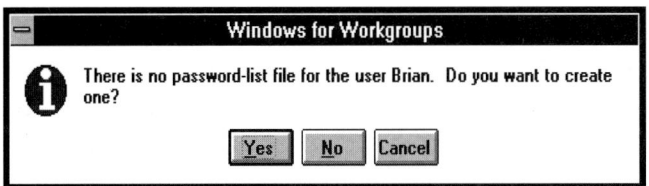

Note
The password-list file records your logon password and other passwords which may be required to connect to shared resources.

Unless you want to be confronted by this screen every time you use WFWG, press the Enter key or use the mouse to click on the **Y**es button. WFWG will then set up a file to record all the passwords you use.

Chapter 1. The Basics

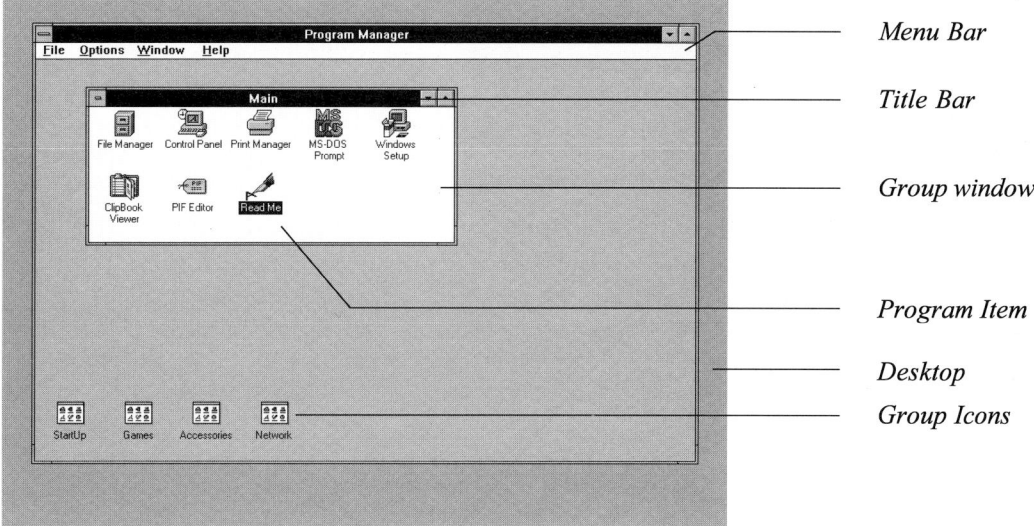

Menu Bar

Title Bar

Group window

Program Item

Desktop

Group Icons

You will then see a screen very similar to the one above, called the Program Manager.

Program Manager consists of several groups of applications: Main, Accessories, Network, Games and Startup. You can also create other new groups of your own.

Application groups are represented by *Group icons* and programs within them by *Program Item icons*. All related programs are grouped together inside a Group icon or a window. The 'picture' of a particular Program item will give you a clue to what the program does. For example, Print Manager will monitor and control the printing of files.

Using Menus/Dialog Boxes

If a menu option is dimmed out, it cannot be used at this particular stage. In this example Move... and Copy... cannot be used as a program item has not been selected.

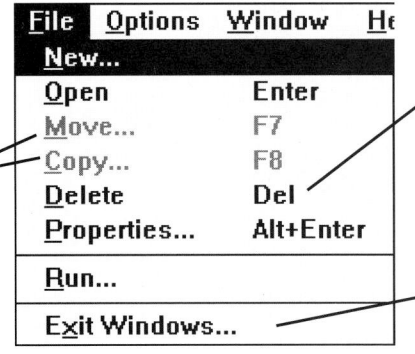

If a key or key combination is listed on the right of the menu, it can be used instead of the menu.

The ellipse (ie ...) indicates that if this option is selected, an associated dialog box will appear.

A tick shows that an option is active. Click on the option to deactivate it.

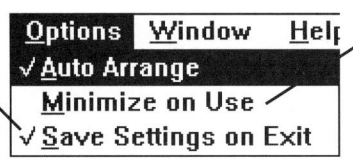

This option is not active as there is no tick next to it. Click on it to activate it.

Radio Buttons - if a bullet is shown next to one of the options, that option has been selected. Only one out of a group of radio buttons can be selected, clicking another radio button automatically turns off the previously selected one.

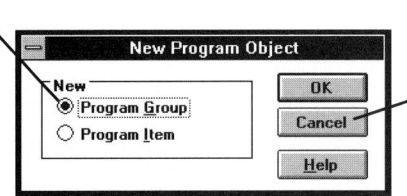

Action buttons - clicking one of these buttons performs the specified function and removes the dialog box from the screen.

Check boxes - options selected contain an 'X'. Click on the box again to deselect it and remove the 'X'. If a dialog box has several check boxes, multiple options can be selected.

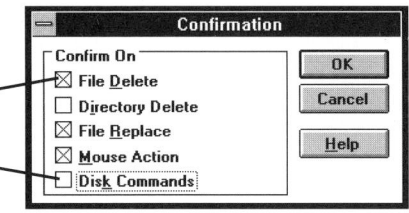

Moving a Window

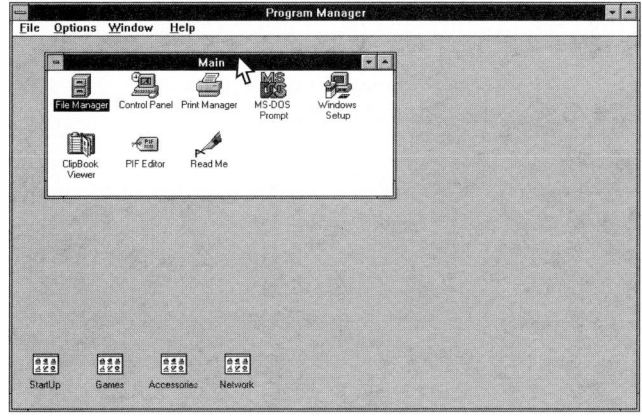

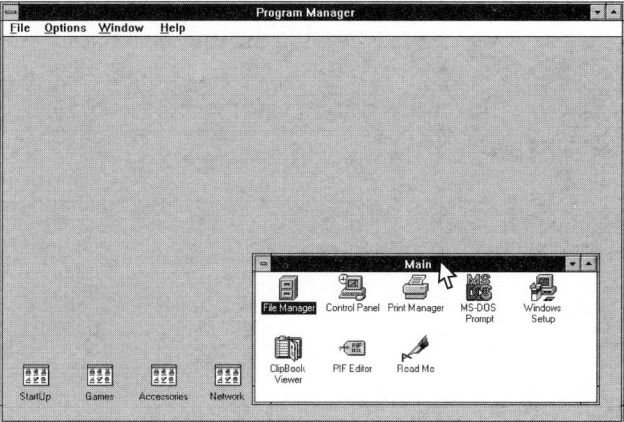

1. Move the mouse pointer over the window's Title Bar.
2. Drag the mouse pointer to a new location.
3. When the window frame is in the correct position, release the mouse button.

Maximising/Restoring Windows

Tip
You can also double-click on the Title Bar of a window to maximise it.

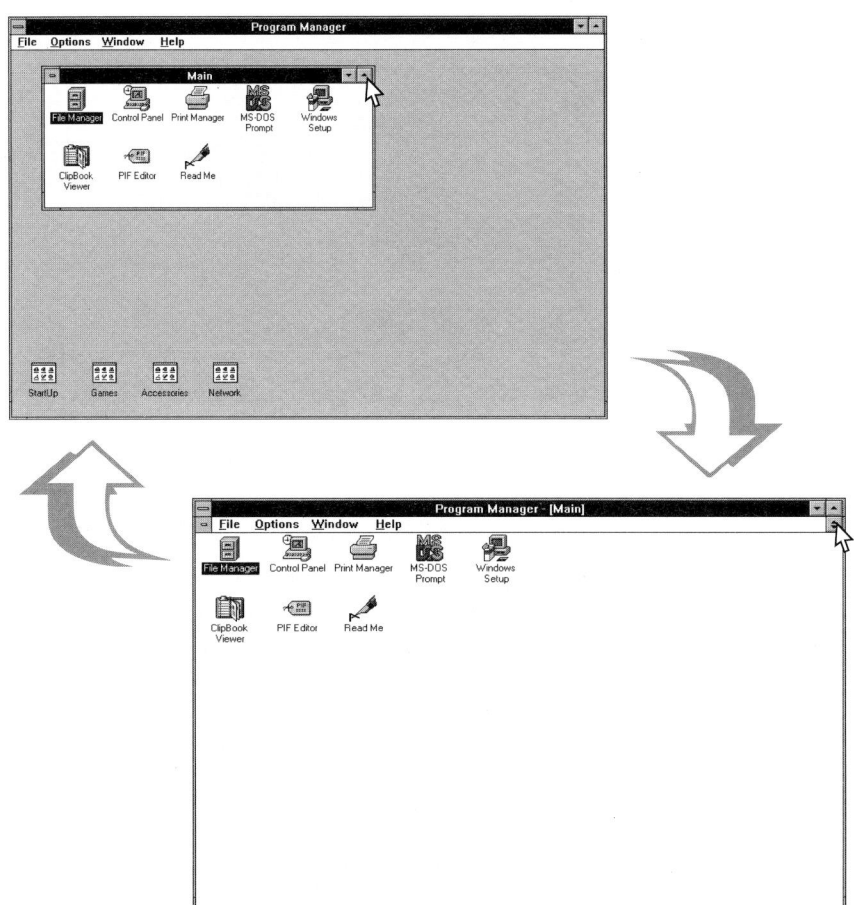

1. Click on the Maximise button to enlarge a window. The window will then occupy the whole screen to provide more working area as shown.

2. Click on the Restore button to reduce or restore the window to its original size.

Minimising/Restoring Windows

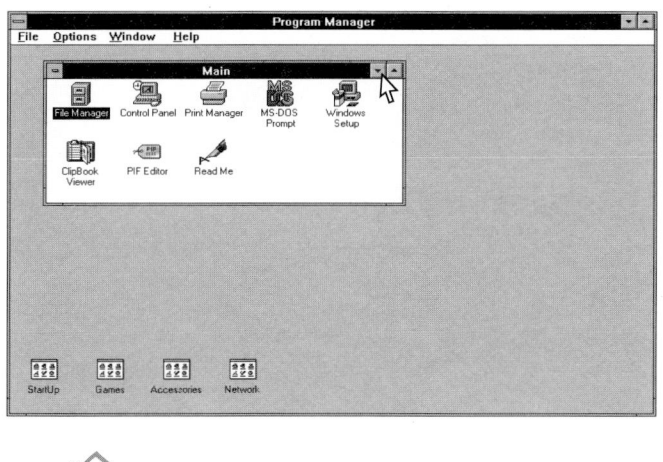

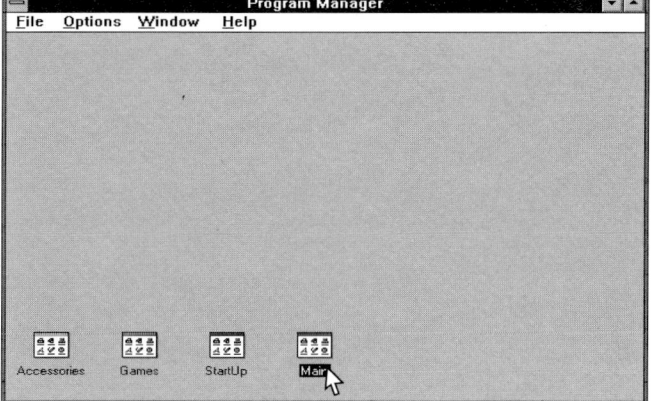

1. Click on the Minimise button to reduce or minimise a window to an icon as shown. Your desktop area will now be cleared and you can use it for other Window applications.

2. Double-click on the icon in quick succession to restore the window to its original size.

Resizing Windows

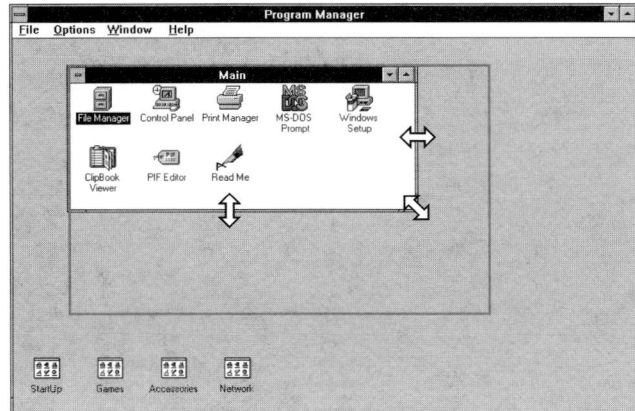

Note
A Group window cannot be extended beyond the Program Manager window.

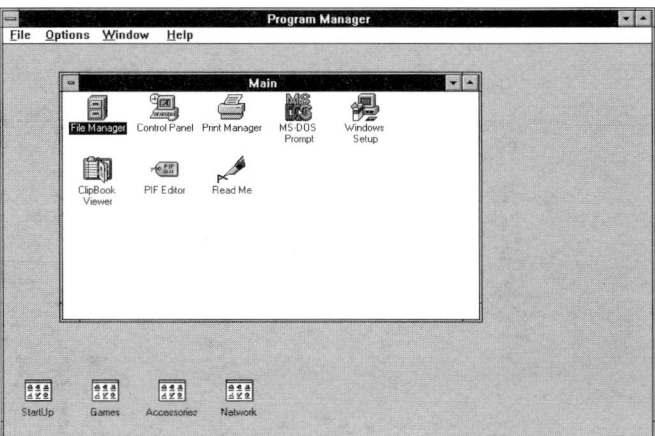

1. Place the mouse arrow on the edge of a window so that it becomes double-headed. To stretch the window horizontally, place the arrow on the left/right edge. To stretch it vertically, place the arrow on the top/bottom edge. To stretch it in both direction at the same time, place the arrow on one of the four corners of a window.

2. When a double-headed arrow is displayed, drag the mouse in the appropriate direction to enlarge or reduce the size.

Rearranging Icons

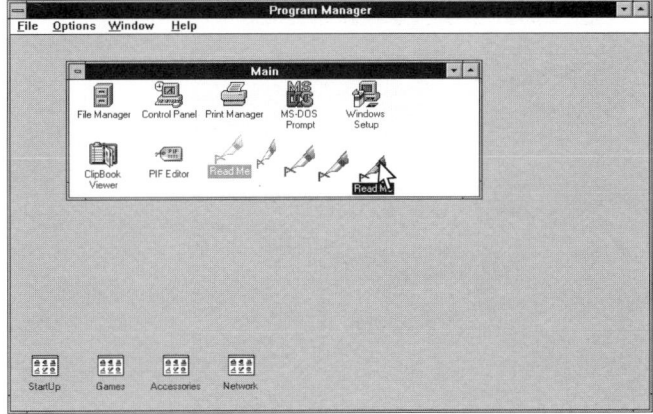

Tip
You can also move an icon from one window to another.

Tip
Press the Ctrl key and at the same time drag an icon with the mouse to make a copy of it.

1. Place the mouse pointer over an icon.

2. Drag the mouse pointer to re-position the icon and then release the button.

Arranging Icons Automatically

1. Click on the **W**indow pull-down menu near the top.

2. Then click on the **A**rrange Icons option within the **W**indow menu. All your icons in a window will now be neatly aligned so that they are equally spaced from each other.

OR

1. Click on the **O**ptions pull-down menu.

2. Then click on **A**uto Arrange option within the **O**ptions menu. Now whenever you re-size a window, all icons within it will be automatically aligned so that the new space is used. A tick here indicates that it has already been selected.

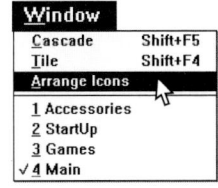

Shortcut
Alt+W, A

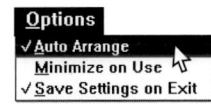

Shortcut
Alt+O, A

Moving between Group Windows

Shortcut
Ctrl+Tab.

1. Click inside any Group window to make it current or active. The title bar for the active window is highlighted.

OR

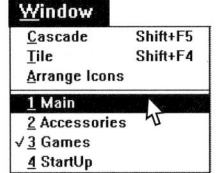

1. Click on the **W**indow menu.

2. Click on one of the Group names from the list at the bottom of the pull-down menu. The currently active window is ticked.

Note
This method is particularly useful when you are trying to access a Group window completely covered with other windows and cannot click on it with a mouse.

Note
Selecting a current Group window (or making it active) is important because many Windows functions can only be operated on the current Group window.

Chapter 1. The Basics

Cascading Group Windows

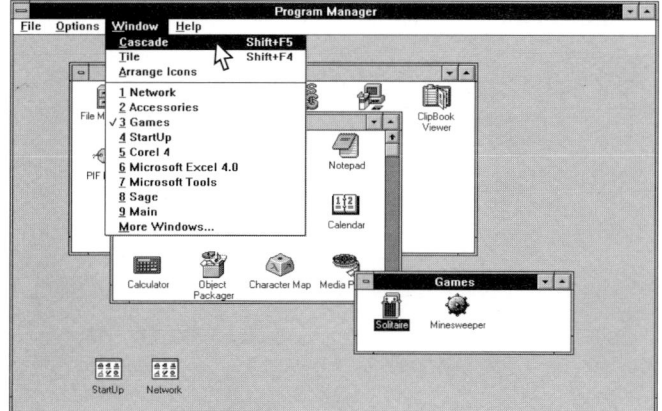

Shortcut
Shift+F5

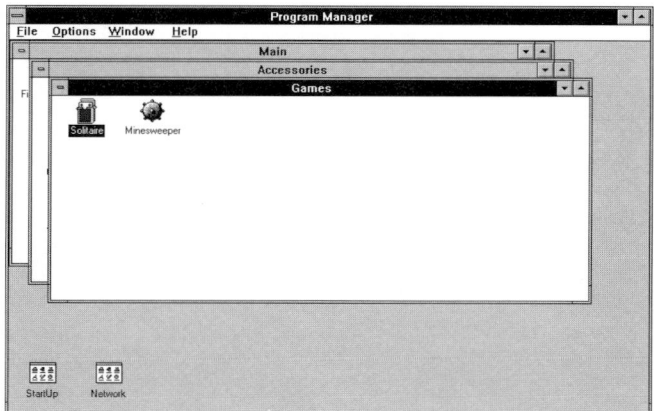

1. Click on the **W**indow menu.

2. Then click on the **C**ascade option to cascade all your Group windows.

Note
Cascading allows you to view all your windows, in case some of them are hidden behind others, and therefore invisible (see also, Tiling Group Windows).

Tiling Group Windows

Shortcut
Shift+F4

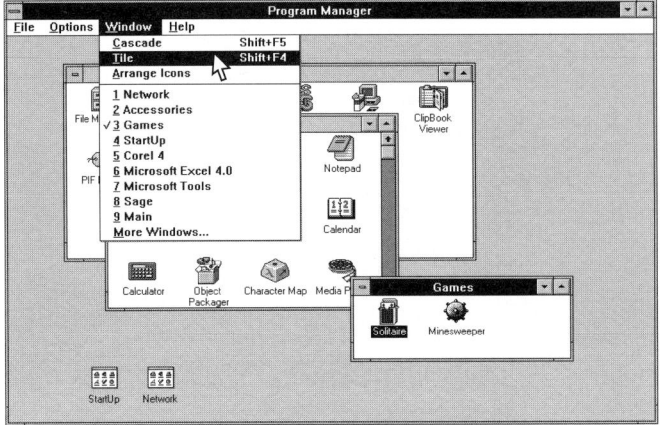

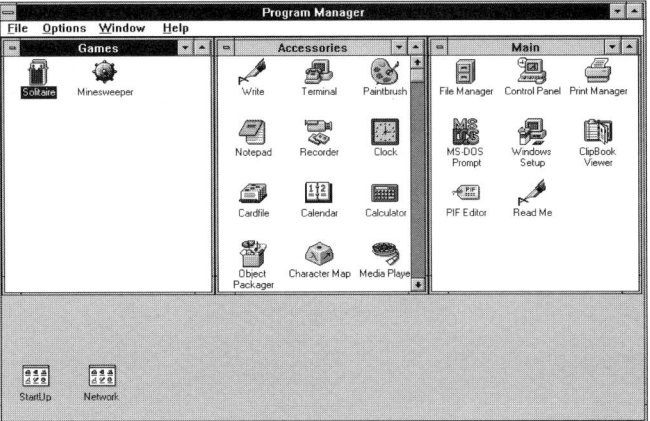

1. Click on the **W**indow menu.

2. Then click on the **T**ile option to tile all your Group windows, starting from the currently active one.

Note
Tiling allows you to view all your windows, in case some of them are hidden behind others, and therefore invisible (see also, Cascading Group Windows).

Scrolling Group Windows

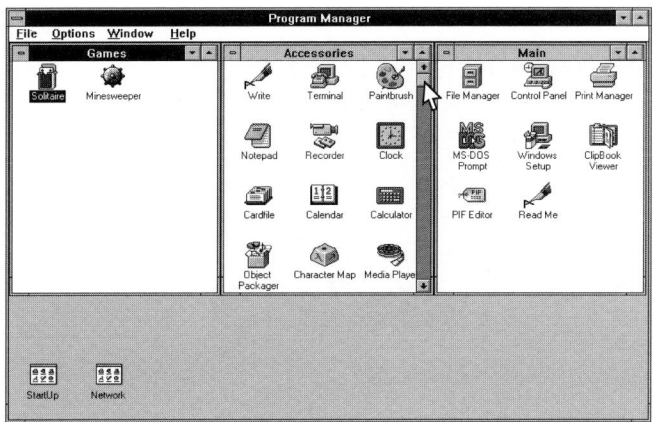

Note
If the size of a Group window is too small to display all the program item icons, scroll bars will appear automatically. This will enable you to view all items in a window. Scroll bars may be vertical (as shown above) to allow up or down scrolling in a window, or horizontal, allowing left or right scrolling. You can also have scroll bars in both direction on the same window at the same time.

1. Click on the scroll arrow to scroll the window in that direction (up, down, left or right).

OR

1. Click on the little square scroll slider in between the scroll arrows.

2. Drag it in the direction you want to scroll.

Closing Windows

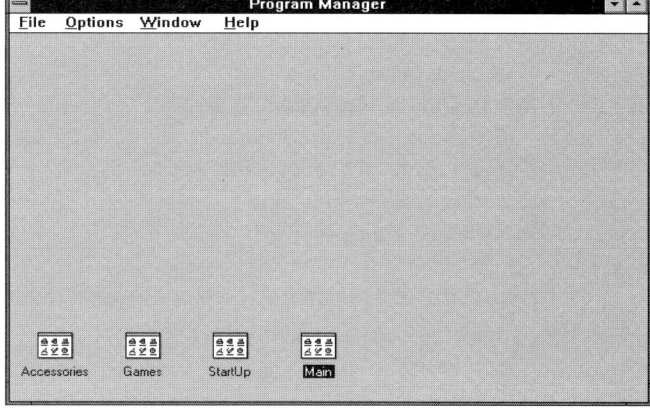

Shortcut
Ctrl+F4

Note
You can also use the Control menu box to perform many of the functions already covered.

1. Double-click on the Control menu box. This is located on the top left-hand side of each window.

OR

1. Click on the Control menu box once to display the Control menu.

2. Click on the **C**lose option.

Using On-screen Help

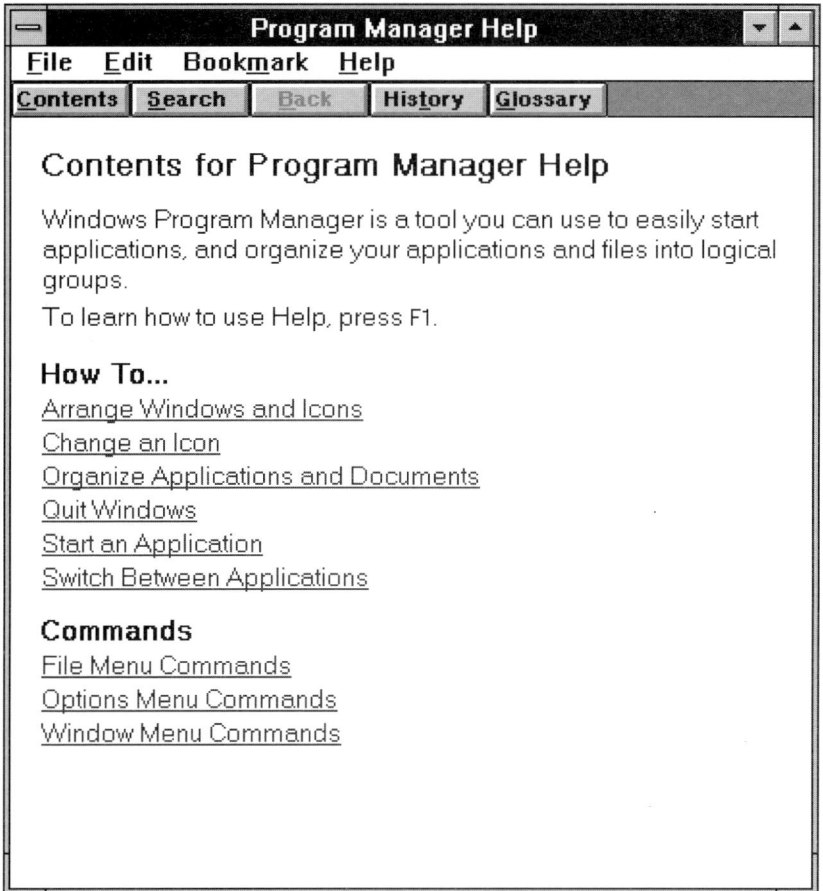
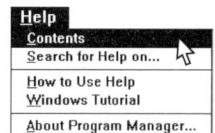

1. Click on the **H**elp menu from the Program Manager window.

2. Click on the **C**ontents option to display a list of very general topics on which help is available.

3. Click on any topic (indicated by underlined text) to obtain detailed help on the subject.

4. Double-click the Control menu box of a Help window to exit from it.

Note

*Click on the **S**earch button from a Help window or select **S**earch for Help on... option from the **H**elp menu to display this dialog box.*

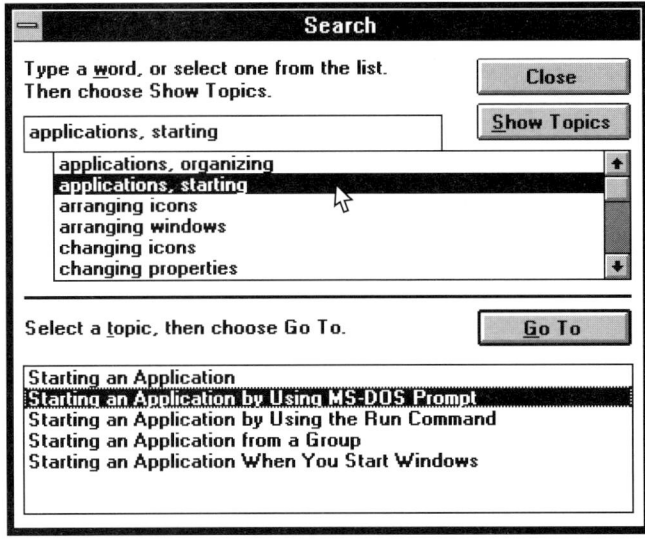

1. Click on the down-scroll arrow to access an alphabetical list of Help topics.

Tip

*Click on **P**rint Topic from the **F**ile menu to get a hard copy of the Help screen displayed.*

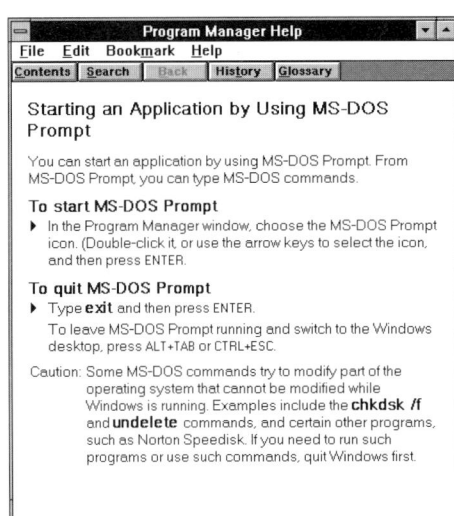

2. Double-click on the desired topic. A more detailed list of topics related to the one chosen is then displayed.

3. Double-click on a topic from this list to display help on it.

Chapter 1. The Basics   23

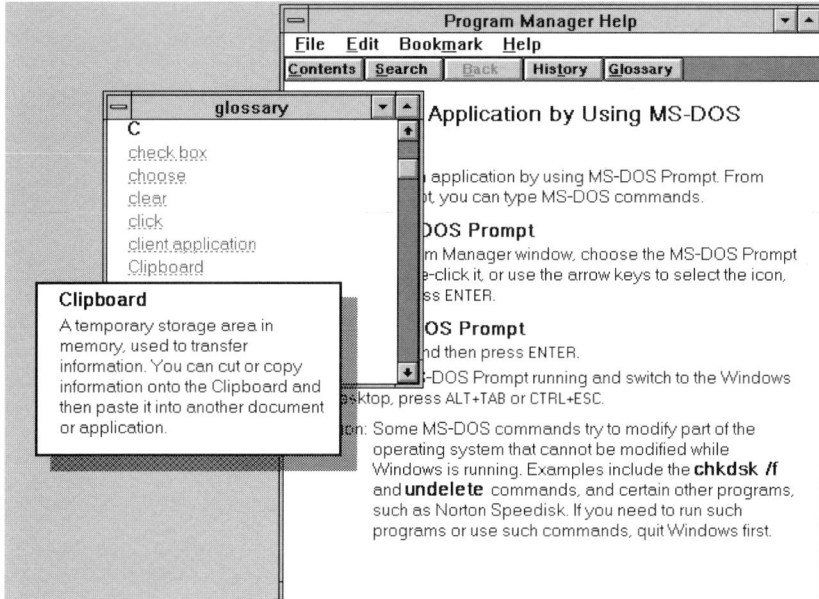

Note
The Glossary explains many Windows terms.

1. Click on the **G**lossary button. An alphabetical list of terms is displayed.

2. Use the scroll-down arrow to view all the terms.

3. Click on the term you want. An explanation will then be displayed in a small pop-up window.

4. To remove the little window, click anywhere, or press any key.

Note
*Click on the **B**ack button to display the previous topic viewed again. Click on the His**t**ory button to display a list of all topics viewed so far. You can double-click on any topic from this list to view it again.*

Invoking Context-sensetive Help

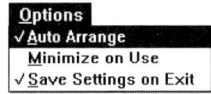
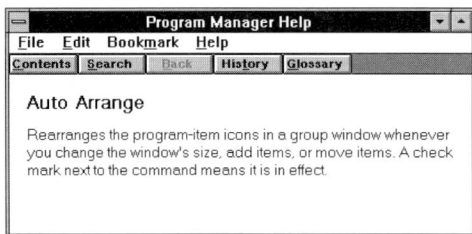

Note

Context-sensitive Help is specific help on the currently selected feature.

1. Select a menu option by highlighting it with the keyboard cursor arrow keys, or display any WFWG dialog box.

2. Press F1 key on your keyboard to display help on the currently active menu option or dialog box.

Starting a Mouse Tutorial

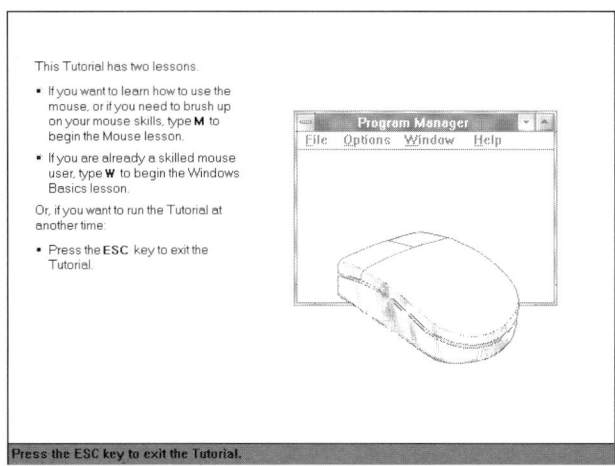

1. Select **W**indows Tutorial from the Help menu.

2. Follow the instructions given. Press the Esc key to exit from the tutorial.

Exiting Windows for Workgroups

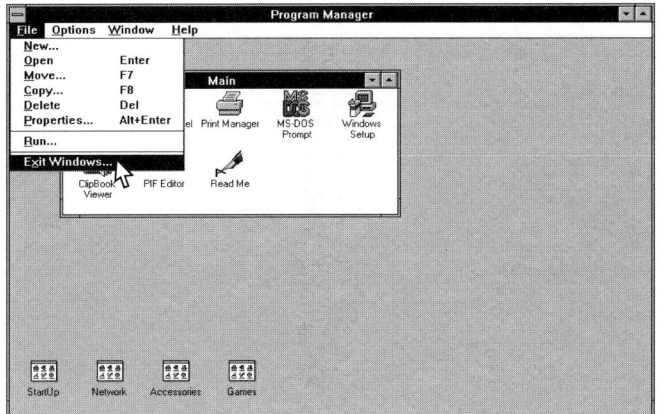

Tip
Another way to exit WFWG is to close the Program Manager window (see Closing Windows).

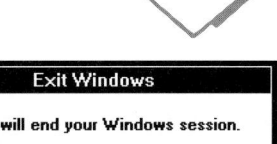

1. Click on the **F**ile menu.

2. Click on E**x**it Windows... option from the **F**ile menu.

3. Click on OK from the Exit Windows dialog box displayed in the middle of the screen. If there are no other users connected to your computer this will bring you to the DOS prompt (C:\>). Click on the Cancel button (or hit ESC key) if you have changed your mind about exiting. If there are any other users connected a warning box will be displayed.

Shortcut
Alt+F,X or Alt+F4

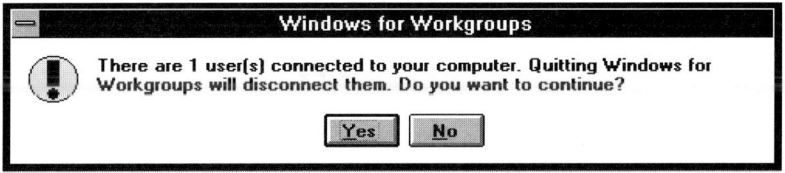

4. If you still want to exit WFWG, click on **Y**es and your computer will bring you to the DOS prompt (C:\>). Click on **N**o (or hit the ESC key) if you have changed your mind about exiting.

Note
*Before exiting WFWG, check the **O**ptions menu to see if the '**S**ave Settings on Exit' is on (ticked). This will save any changes you have made to the arrangement of icons and Group windows in the current session.*

CHAPTER 2
Working with Applications

THIS CHAPTER COVERS

- Setting up Program Groups
- Setting up Programs
- Setting up several Programs
- Setting up Non-Windows Programs
- Starting an Application
- Working with several Programs
- Using the Task List
- Using the Clipboard
- Saving the Clipboard
- Displaying ClipBook Pages
- Copying ClipBook Pages into the Clipboard
- Deleting ClipBook Pages
- Sharing ClipBook Pages
- Unsharing ClipBook Pages
- Connecting to a shared ClipBook
- Disconnecting from a shared ClipBook
- Exiting to the MS-DOS Prompt
- Automating Startups
- Organising your Desktop

in easy Steps

Setting up Program Groups

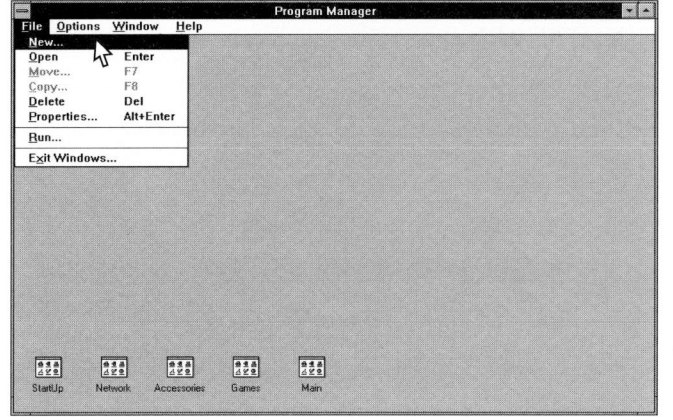

Note
Similar types of Programs or Applications may be grouped together under one Program Group.

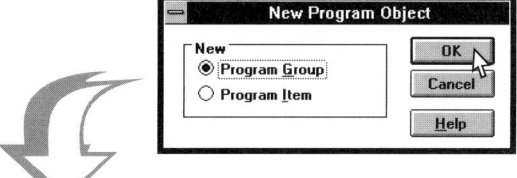

Note
Windows where you are expected to provide information are called dialog boxes.

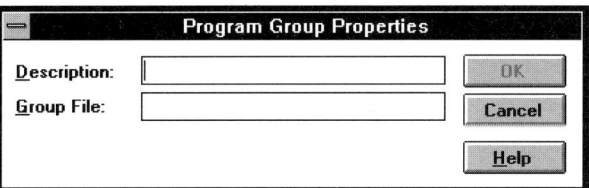

1. Click on **F**ile from the menu bar.

2. Click on **N**ew from the pull-down menu to display a New Program Object dialog box.

3. Click on the Program **G**roup option button if it is not already selected with a dark dot inside the circle.

4. Click on OK. The Program Group Properties dialog box will be displayed.

Tip
You can change the Group Description later by selecting Properties... from the File menu.

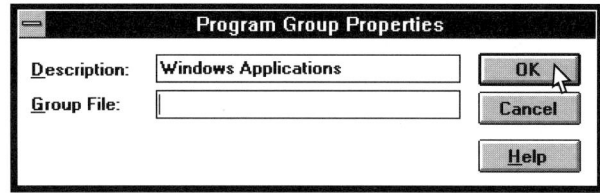

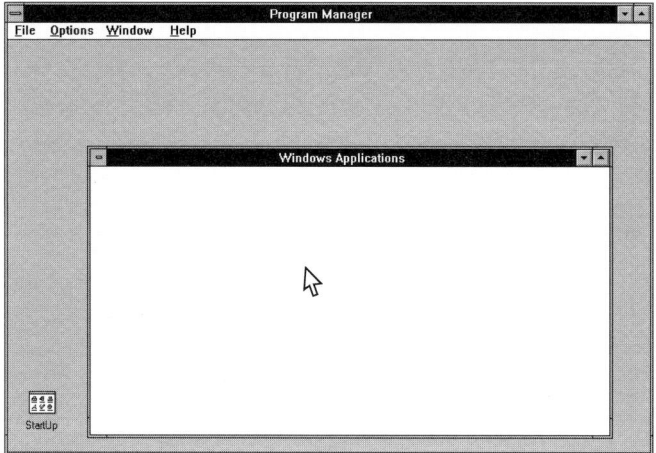

Note
If you want to place new program item icons in your group window, see the next section.

5. Type a name for your new Group. This will be displayed on the title bar of the new group window.

6. It is optional to type a file name for the Group in the next box. WFWG will create it automatically from the first eight letters of **D**escription and an extension of GRP.

7. Click on OK. A new group window will then be displayed.

Tip
*To delete a program group, select it and then choose **D**elete from the **F**ile menu.*

Note
You can move and size this new group window as shown in Chapter 1. You can also place Program item icons in this window from other group windows. Simply drag the icons, one at a time, from one window to another using the mouse - it is same as rearranging icons within a window, as shown in Chapter 1.

Chapter 2. Working with Applications

Setting up Programs

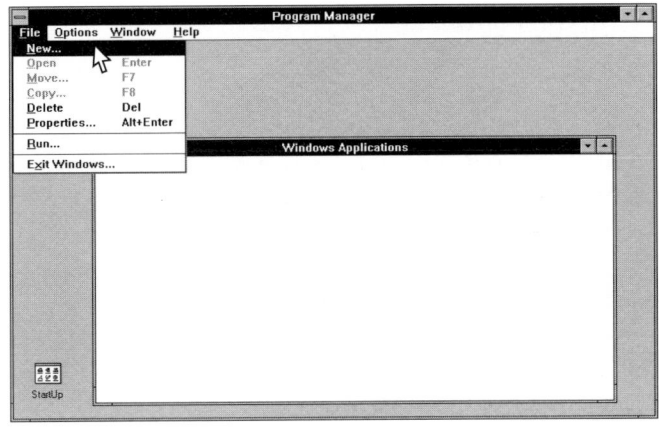

1. Activate the group you want to create a new program item in by clicking on it

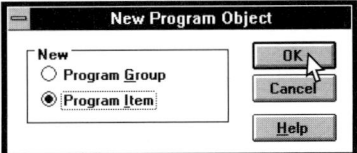

Shortcut

Miss out previous steps and get to this box straight away by holding down the Alt key and double clicking in a blank area of a group.

2. Click on New from the pull-down File menu to display a New Program Object dialog box.

3. Click on the Program Item option button if it is not already selected with a dark dot inside the circle.

4. Click on OK. The Program Item Properties dialog box will be displayed.

5. Type a description of your new program in the **D**escription box.

6. Type the main program file name used to run the new program in the **C**ommand Line box. It is usually an EXE file (for example WINWORD.EXE). You should also include the path to this file.

Tip

*If you do not know the path, click on the **B**rowse... button to list files and directories. Then, click on the appropriate directory (you can double-click on the root directory (C:\) to display main directories). When you have found your program file, double-click on it to select it and to automatically include the path and the name of the file in the **C**ommand Line.*

Tip

*You can use the **R**un Minimized option to keep most of your desktop area clear, to work on something else right after you have started your application.*

7. The rest of the boxes are optional. The **W**orking directory, if specified, is made current when you run the application. The **S**hortcut Key (e.g. Ctrl+Shift+any character) is useful if you are going to run the application often and prefer to quickly get into it using a combination of keys. The **R**un Minimized box, if selected, will reduce the application to an icon when you start it.

8. Click on the OK button. You should now see the new program icon appear inside your group window.

Tip

*To delete a program item icon, highlight the icon and then choose **D**elete from the **F**ile menu. This will not delete the actual programs but just the icons.*

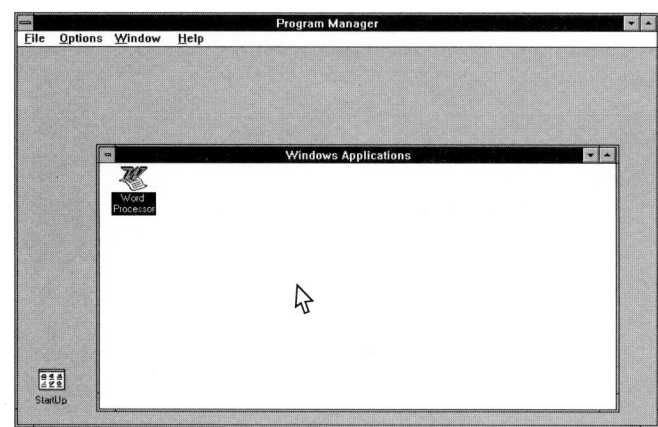

Setting up several Programs

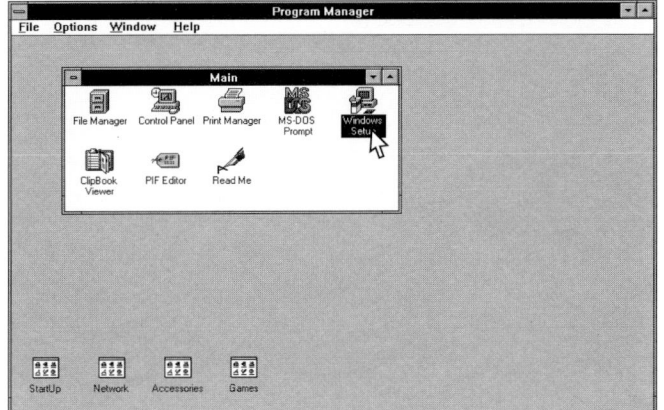

Tip
If you have many programs to add, save time by using Windows Setup.

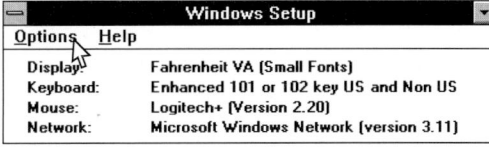

1. Double-click on Windows Setup icon. This will display your main setup under WFWG.

2. Click on **O**ptions menu from the Windows Setup box.

3. Select **S**et Up Applications... from the pull-down menu.

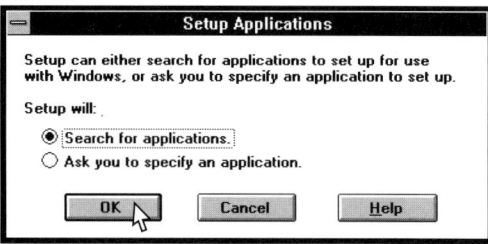

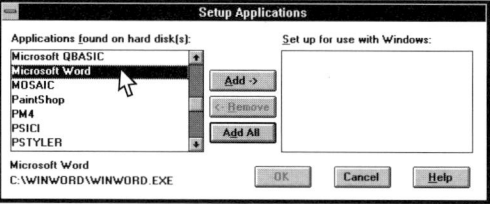

Shortcut

Double-click on programs to add them quickly to the list on the right, or click on Add All to select all of them.

4. From the Set Up Applications dialog box, select Search for Applications and click on OK. WFWG will then prompt you to tell it where it should search for applications: the whole hard disk, or only from directories specified in a path command.

5. A list of programs found are displayed, a few at a time, in a box on the left. Click on programs required and then click on the **A**dd button.

6. Click on OK. Your selected programs will all be set up in a new Applications group window. From here you can easily move them to other groups, if required.

Setting up Non-Windows Programs

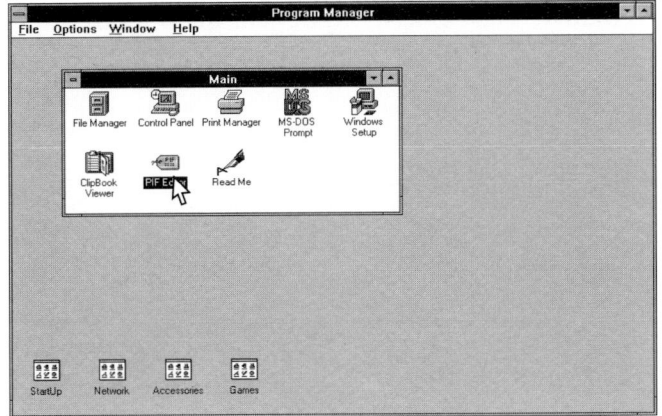

Note
PIF stands for Program Information File. It is recommended that you use the PIF editor to set up any DOS applications that you want to run from WFWG.

1. Double-click on the PIF Editor icon from the Main group.

2. In the PIF editor, first type the name of the main DOS file which executes the program. e.g. SAGE.EXE

3. Tab to the next box and type in a description. This will appear later as the Windows title for your DOS program.

4. Type in the directory (including path) where the DOS EXE file exists.

5. Click on **W**indowed (Display Usage) near the bottom if you want your DOS application to run inside a window.

6. Click on the **F**ile menu.

7. Choose Save **A**s... from the pull-down menu.

8. Then from the Save As dialog box, type a file name representing your DOS program (e.g. SAGE) with a file type of PIF.

9. Close the PIF Editor window by double-clicking on its control box.

10. Follow the same procedure as setting up programs except, in the **C**ommand Line under the Program Item Properties dialog box, type the name and path of the PIF file you saved in step 8.

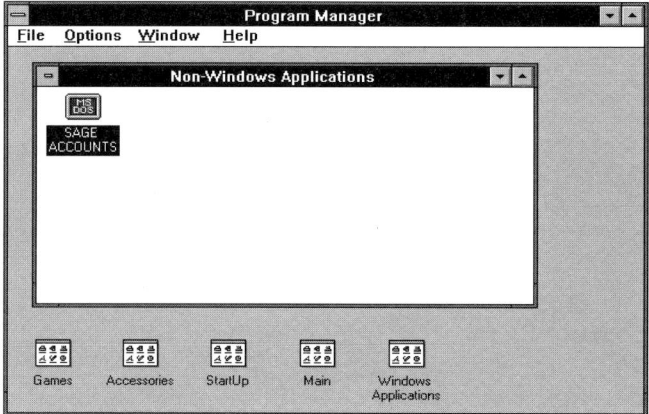

Starting an Application

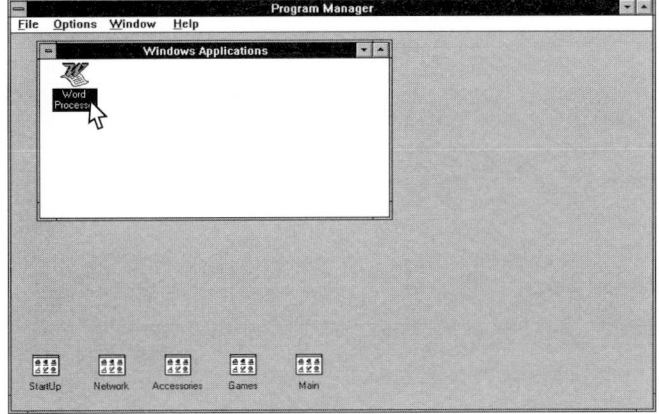

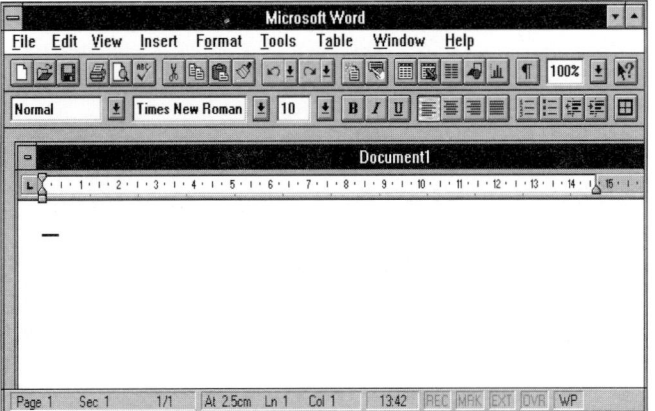

Tip
You can also start a program by double-clicking on its main EXE file from the file listing in File Manager (see next Chapter).

1.   Double-click on the Program item icon.

OR

1.   Click on the **F**ile menu.

2.   Select **R**un... to display the Run dialog box.

3.   Type the name of the program (including path) in the Run dialog box and click on OK.

Working with several Programs

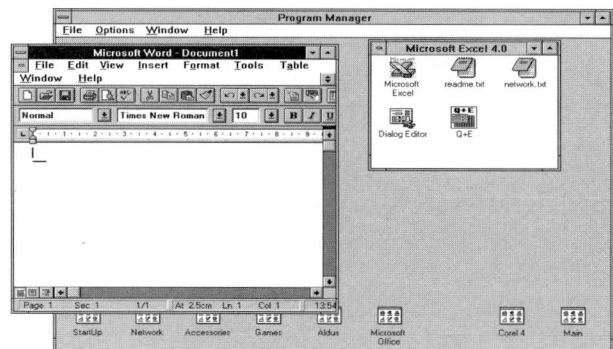

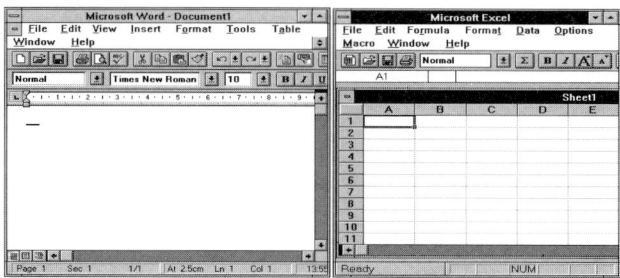

Tip
Refer to Chapter 1 if you need help with resizing and moving windows.

1. Double-click on an application icon (e.g. Word). Resize and move the Word window to one side of the desktop.

2. Double-click on another application icon (e.g. Excel). Size and position its window too.

3. Click on the Minimize button for the Program Manager to reduce it to an icon at the bottom of the screen.

Shortcut
Alt+Tab

4. Now you can work on both applications at the same time. Click on the appropriate window to switch to it.

Using the Task List

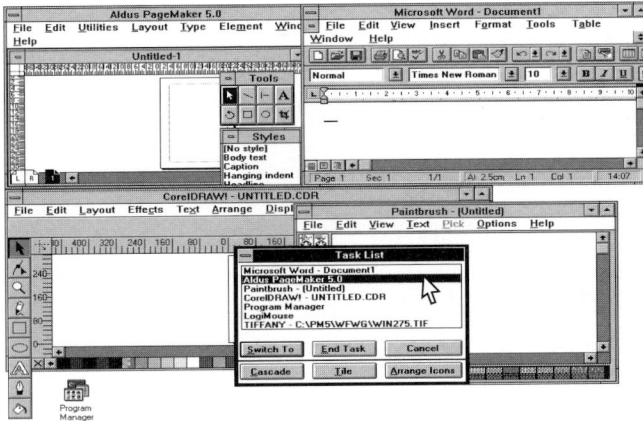

Note
A task list is used to display all your running programs and switch between them.

1. Start several programs, size their windows and position them on your desktop.

2. Press Ctrl+Esc to display the Task List.

3. Click on a program name from the Task List to select it. Then click on the **S**witch To button to make that program current. It will move to the foreground.

4. Click on **T**ile button to display all program windows so that they are equally sized as shown below.

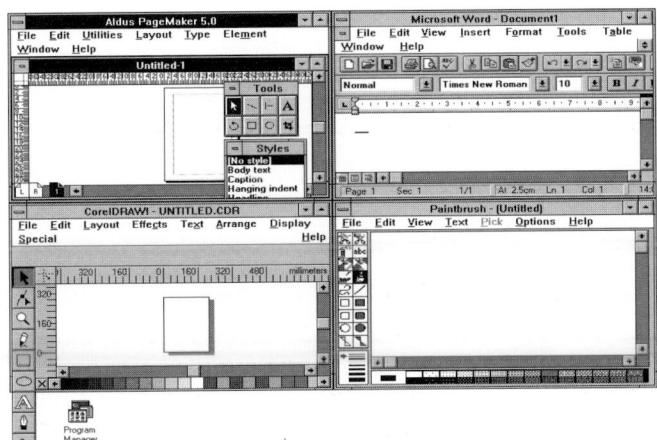

Shortcut
Double-click on the background area of a desktop not covered by any windows to open a Task List.

Shortcut
Alt+Esc

5. Click on **C**ascade button to overlap all program windows so that at least their title bars are showing.

6. Click on **E**nd Task button to close the selected program window.

7. If all your program windows are minimized to icons, click on **A**rrange Icons to neatly arrange them in order at the bottom of the desktop.

Shortcut

Esc

8. Click on Cancel to exit from the Task List.

Using the Clipboard

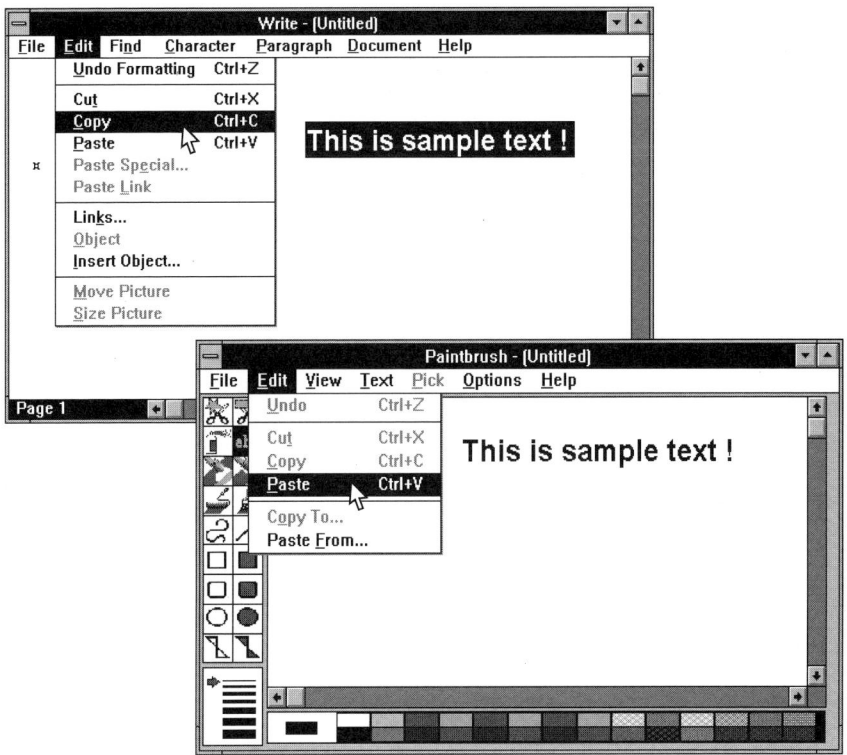

Note
A Clipboard is a temporary storage area. It is used to transfer information between applications and within the same document.

1. As an example, start the Write application.

2. Highlight a piece of text by dragging the mouse from start to finish.

3. Click on the **E**dit menu and choose either Cu**t** or **C**opy options. Your highlighted text is now saved in a clipboard.

4. Now start another Windows application, say Paintbrush.

5. Choose the text tool (abc) and click in an area on screen.

6. Select **P**aste from the **E**dit menu. The contents of the clipboard will then be dumped on the screen.

Tip
Press the Print Screen key from the keyboard to copy the whole screen into the clipboard.

Saving the Clipboard

Note

The contents of the Clipboard will be overwritten when other objects are copied into it and lost when the machine is switched off. Therefore, if the contents need to be saved or shared by other users on the network, they need to be stored as ClipBook pages.

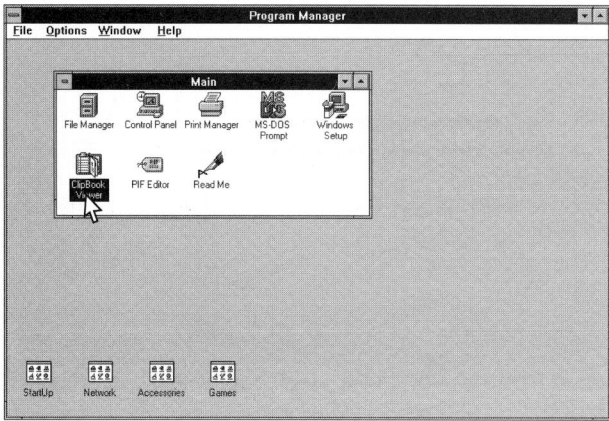

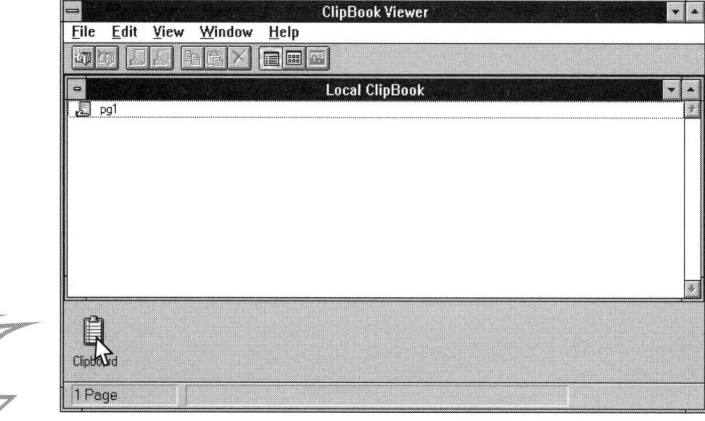

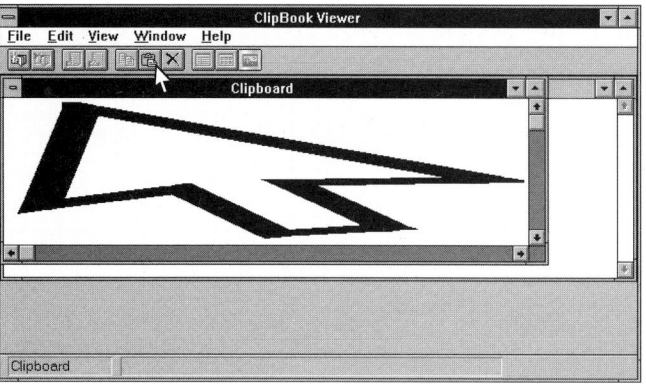

Chapter 2. Working with Applications

1. Double-click on the ClipBook Viewer icon in the Main group. This will display the Local ClipBook.

2. Double-click on the Clipboard icon at the bottom of the ClipBook Viewer screen to display the Clipboard.

3. Select the Paste button on the Toolbar (or **P**aste from the **E**dit menu) to paste the Clipboard contents into the Local ClipBook. The Paste dialog box is then displayed.

4. In the **P**age Name box type a name for the new ClipBook page and click on OK.

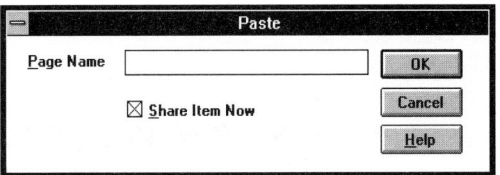

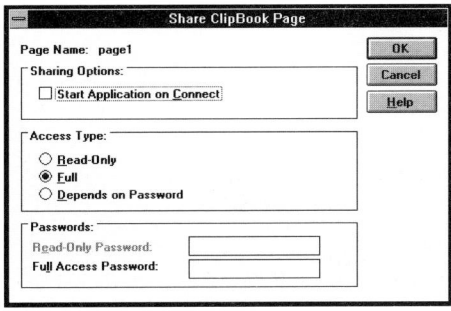

5. If the **S**hare Item Now check box is selected, then the Share ClipBook Page dialog box is displayed. Here you can make your ClipBook page available to others on the network. Choose **F**ull access or **R**ead-only access and a password, if required.

6. Click on OK.

Displaying ClipBook Pages

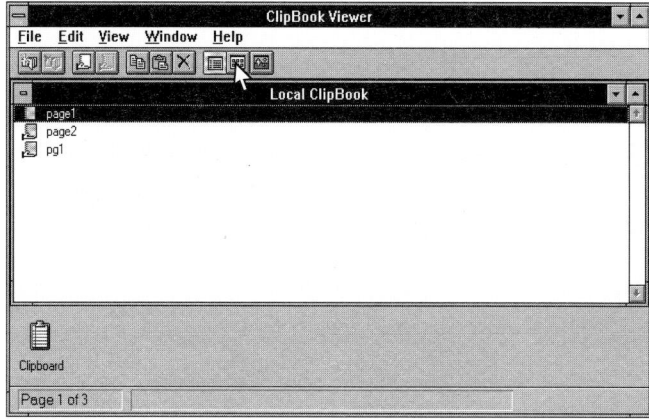

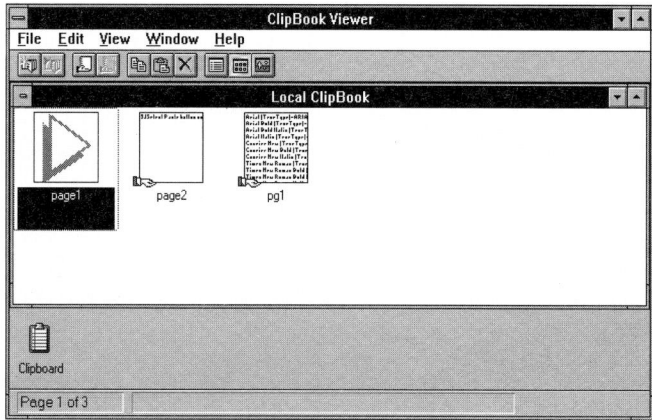

Tip
ClipBook pages with a 'hand' symbol are shared pages - see Sharing ClipBook Pages for details on how to do this.

Thumbnails

Full Page

Table of Contents

1. Click on the Thumbnails button (or select Thumb**n**ails on the **V**iew menu). Small sketches of the ClipBook pages will be displayed.

2. To select a full page view, click on the Full Page button or select **F**ull Page from the **V**iew menu.

3. The third view option is a listing of the titles of pages which is obtained by clicking on the Table of Contents button or selecting Table of **C**ontents from the **V**iew menu.

Copying ClipBook Pages into the Clipboard

1. From the ClipBook Viewer, click on the page required.

2. Click on the Paste button on the Toolbar (or choose Paste from the Edit menu). The contents of the ClipBook page will be pasted into the Clipboard.

Note
Copying a ClipBook page into the Clipboard allows you to use the contents of the page in your Windows applications (use Paste from the Edit menu within the application).

Deleting ClipBook Pages

1. To delete a ClipBook page, select the page in ClipBook Viewer by clicking on it and highlighting it.

2. Click on the Delete button on the Toolbar (or choose Delete from the Edit menu). A Delete dialog box will appear as shown.

Tip
You can also use this button to clear the contents of the Clipboard.

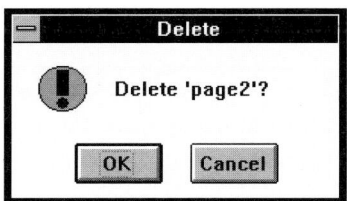

3. Click on OK and the ClipBook page will be deleted.

Sharing ClipBook Pages

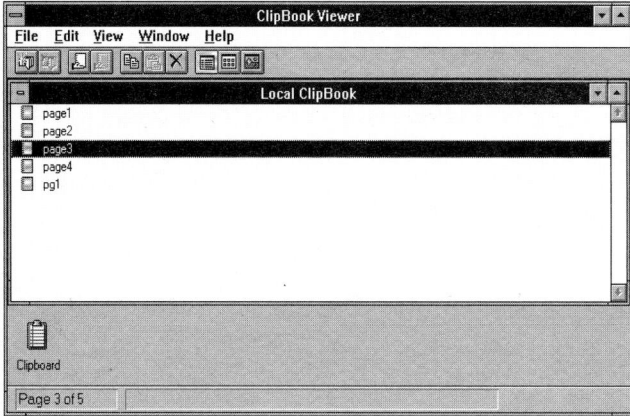

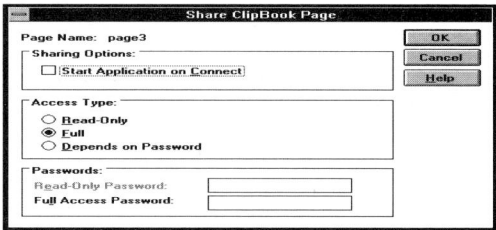

1. From the ClipBook Viewer, select the page you want to share and click on the Share button on the Toolbar (or select Share... from the File menu). A dialog box appears.

2. Choose Full or Read-only access and a Password if required and also check the box 'Start Application on Connection' if required. Then click on OK and the page will appear in the ClipBook with a shared page icon.

Unsharing ClipBook Pages

1. In ClipBook Viewer click on the page you want to unshare.

2. Click on the Stop Sharing button in the Toolbar or select Stop Sharing from the File Menu.

Connecting to a shared ClipBook

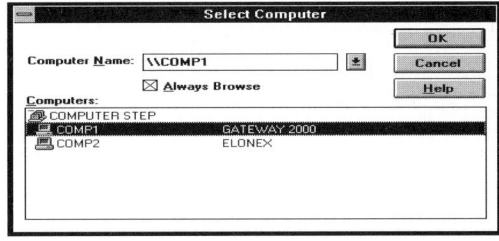

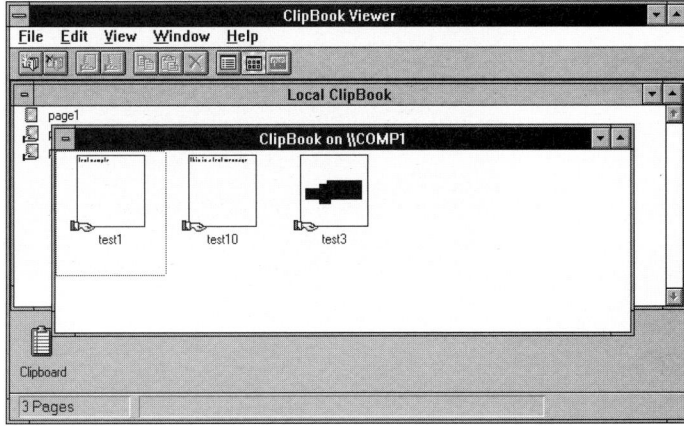

1. Click on the Connect button on the Toolbar or choose Connect... from the File Menu. The Select Computer dialog box is displayed.

2. In the Computer Name box type the name of the computer you wish to connect to. Click on OK.

3. The ClipBook of the selected computer will be displayed.

Disconnecting from a shared ClipBook

1. Click on the ClipBook you wish to diconnect from and click on the Disconnect button on the Toolbar (or select Disconnect from the File menu).

Exiting to the MS-DOS Prompt

MS-DOS Prompt

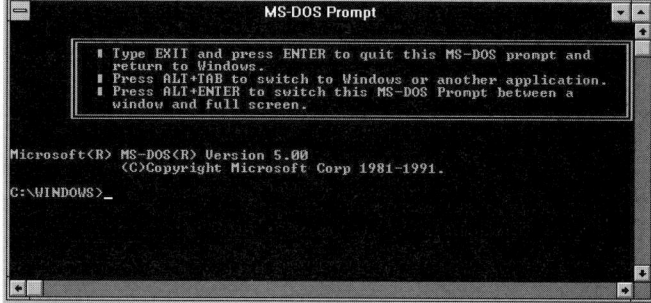

Warning
Some DOS commands should not be issued when WFWG is running. e.g. CHKDSK /F and UNDELETE.

1. Double-click on the MS-DOS Prompt icon in the Main group.

2. When the MS-DOS Prompt is displayed (C:\>) you can type any DOS commands or run DOS applications.

3. Press Alt+Enter keys to toggle between the full-screen MS-DOS Prompt screen and windowed. The MS-DOS Prompt screen is a Non-Windows application. Its display is controlled by DOSPRMPT.PIF file. You can edit this file using the PIF Editor as discussed under the section, Setting up Non-Windows Programs.

4. Type EXIT at the MS-DOS Prompt to return to WFWG.

Automating Startups

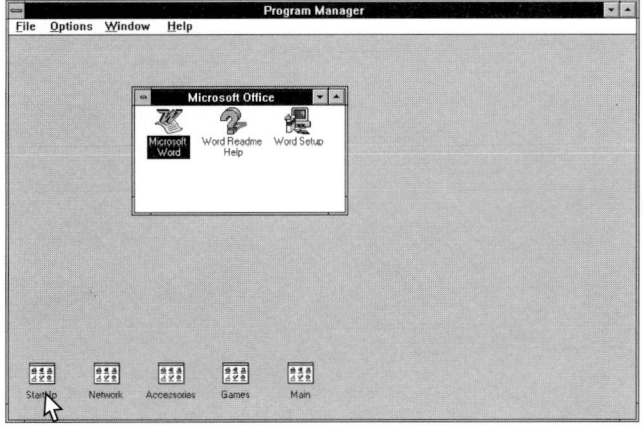

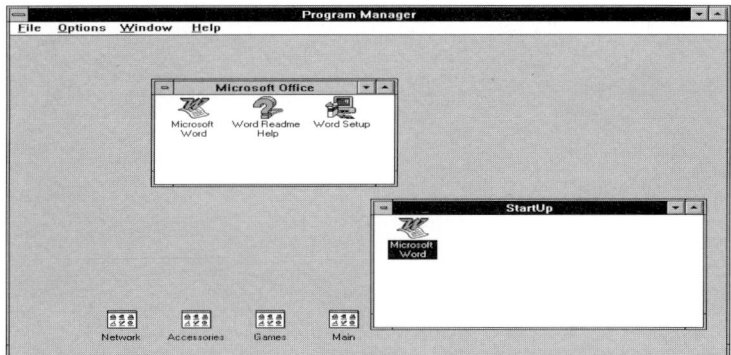

1. Double-click on the StartUp group icon to open it into a window.

2. Drag an application icon (e.g. Microsoft Word) to the StartUp group window. If you press the Ctrl key at the same time as dragging, you will create a copy of the icon which is moved. The original icon stays at the same place.

3. Now, whenever you start WFWG, any program(s) in the StartUp group will start automatically. This is a useful feature for program(s) you use frequently.

Organising your Desktop

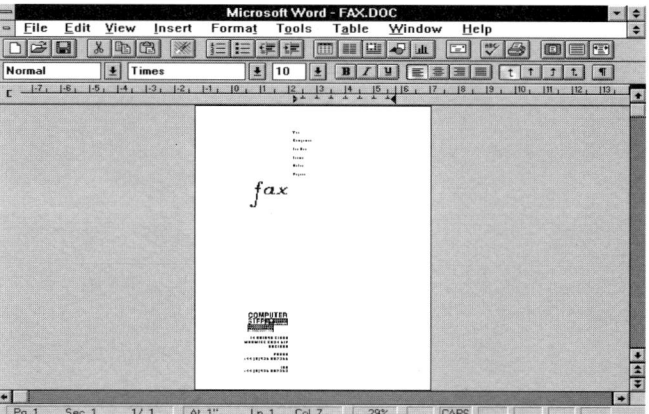

1. Create new groups and program items as described earlier in this chapter. Also organise these on your desktop as required by moving and sizing windows (described in Chapter 1).

2. You can create more meaningful group names, like "Office Duties" as in our example.

3. Customise program icons to functions you regularly perform. For example Fax, Letter and Minutes may all

Chapter 2. Working with Applications

use the same word processor program. However, you can set up your system so that a document or a template is opened automatically, as appropriate for each function.

This can be set when you create a new program by typing the appropriate document name after the program name in the **C**ommand Line box. You can alter it later if you wish by choosing **P**roperties from the **F**ile menu. In our example, note that the document FAX.DOC is used.

4. Click on the Change **I**con button from the Program Item Properties dialog box to select suitable program icons for different purposes.

5. In the Change Icon dialog box, use the program PROGMAN.EXE in the **F**ile Name box to display a range of icons you choose from. It is usually found in the

WINDOWS directory. However, to search for it, click on the **B**rowse button and then click on various directories until you find this file. Double-click on the file from a file list to automatically insert the correct path and file name in the **F**ile Name box.

6. Click on the Scroll arrows to see the choice of icons.

7. Click on the desired icon. It will then be highlighted.

8. Click on the OK button in the Change Icon dialog box and then again in the Program Item Properties dialog box.

CHAPTER 3
Managing your Files

This Chapter Covers

- Starting File Manager
- Splitting Tree/Directory Window
- Viewing Tree/Directory
- Viewing more Information on Files
- Sorting Files
- Working with Multiple Windows
- Changing the Screen Font
- Changing Disk Drives
- Changing Directories
- Expanding Directory Branches
- Creating New Directories
- Sharing your Directories
- Unsharing your Directories
- Connecting to a Shared Directory
- Seeing who is using your Directories
- Disconnecting from a Shared Directory
- Selecting Files
- Copying/Moving Files or Directories
- Deleting Files or Directories
- Undeleting Files or Directories
- Renaming Files or Directories
- Searching for Files
- Changing File Attributes
- Associating Files to Applications
- Starting Applications from Files
- Formatting a Disk
- Labelling a Disk
- Copying a Disk
- Scanning for Viruses
- Backing up your Hard Disk

in easy steps

Chapter 3. Managing your Files

Starting File Manager

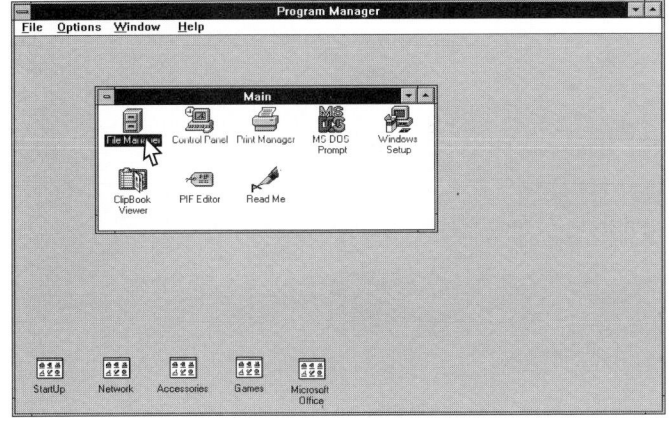

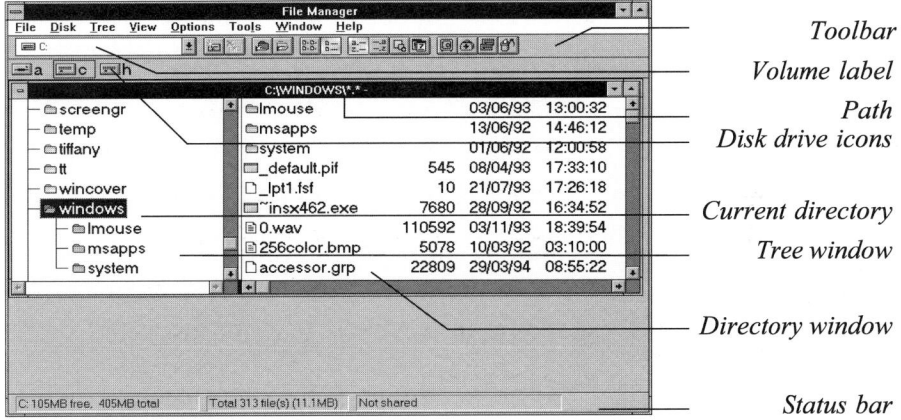

Toolbar
Volume label
Path
Disk drive icons
Current directory
Tree window
Directory window
Status bar

1. Double-click on the File Manager icon in the Main group.

Note
These icons represent directories, programs and files in File Manager.

Parent Directory	Directory/ Sub-directory	Document File	Hidden/ System File	Program File	Other Files	Shared Directory

Splitting Tree/Directory Window

1. Move the mouse pointer on the edge between the Tree and the Directory windows. The pointer will then change its shape as shown.

2. Drag the mouse to the right or the left. A dark vertical bar will move on the screen as you move the mouse.

3. Click on the mouse to re-establish a new border between the two windows. This allows you to have a larger display area for either the Tree window or the Directory window.

OR

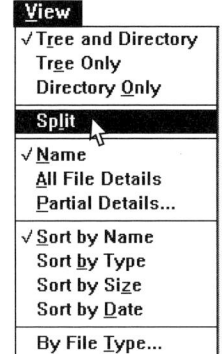

1. Click on the View menu.

2. Click on the Split option from the pull-down View menu. A dark vertical bar will be displayed right away.

3. Move the vertical bar to the left to increase the space for the Directory window and decrease the space for the Tree window. Move it to the right for the opposite effect.

4. Once the bar is in the desired position, click the mouse button to change the display.

Viewing Tree/Directory

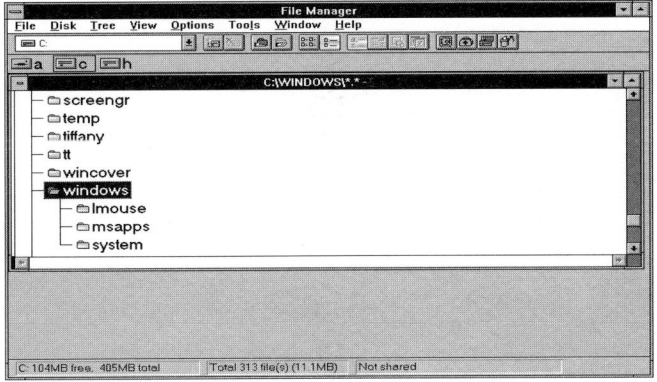 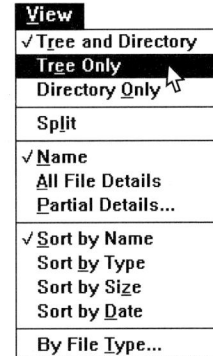

1. Click on the **V**iew menu.

2. Click on the Tr**ee** Only option to display just the tree of directories in the window space.

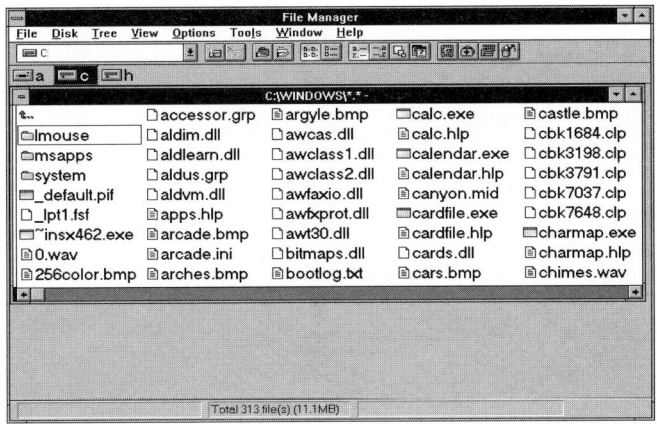 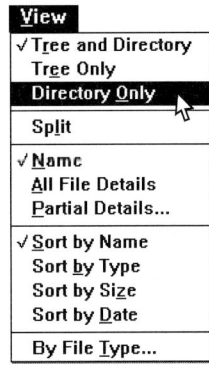

1. Click on the **V**iew menu.

2. Click on the Directory **O**nly option to display just the files from a selected directory in the window space.

Viewing more Information on Files

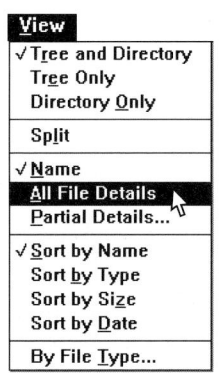

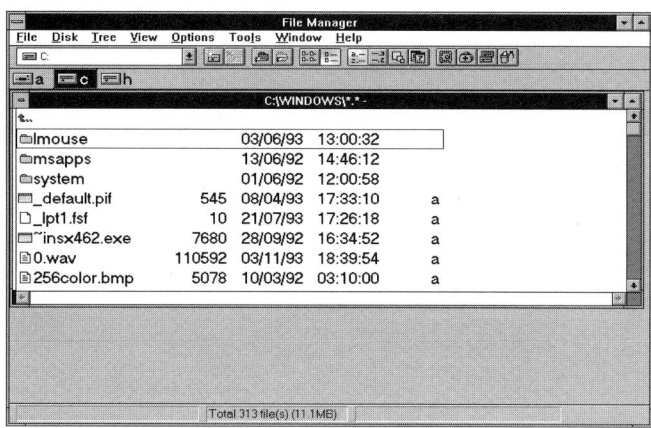

1. Click on the **A**ll File Details option from the **V**iew menu (or click on the All File Details button on the Toolbar) to view file names, sizes, dates and times the files were last modified, and the file attributes - in that order.

Tip
Clicking on the Name button on the Toolbar restores the name only display.

Note
File attributes are:
h *for* **hidden**
s *for* **system**
a *for* **archive**
r *for* **read-only**.
See Changing File Attributes, later in this Chapter for more information.

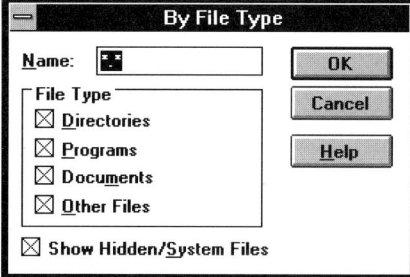

Tip
*You can view files by file type. Select By File **T**ype... from the **V**iew menu. Then choose from **D**irectories, **P**rograms, Doc**u**ments and **O**ther Files by clicking on one or more of the relevant check boxes. Click on the Show Hidden/ **S**ystem Files check box to view any hidden or system files that may exist in the directory window.*

Tip
*You can choose **P**artial Details... from the **V**iew menu and click only on the file information you want displayed (e.g. Size).*

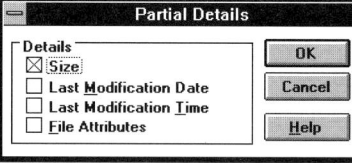

Sorting Files

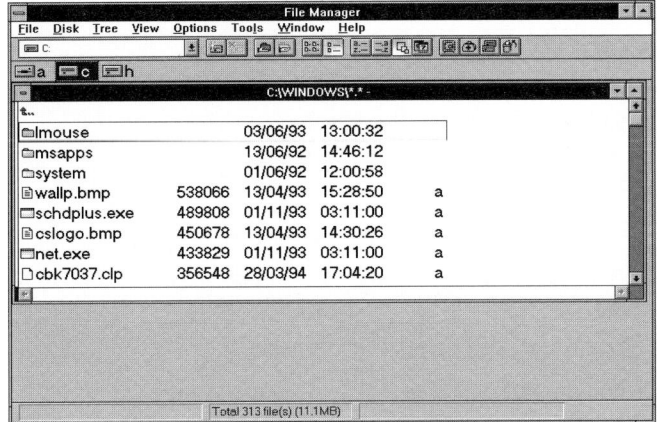

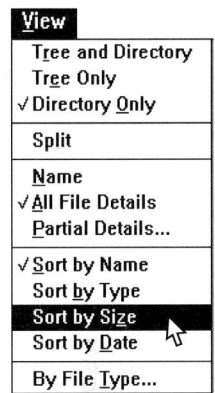

1. Click on the View menu.

2. By default, Sort by Name option is ticked. Therefore, all files are sorted alphabetically by file name. Click on another Sort by attribute to sort files in a different order. Here, Sort by Size displays all files in size order, displaying the largest file first.

Note
Sub-directories are always displayed before files.

OR

1. Click on the appropriate Toolbar button.

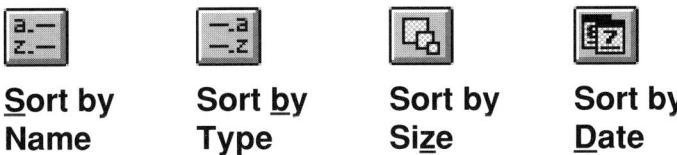

Sort by Name   **Sort by Type**   **Sort by Size**   **Sort by Date**

Working with Multiple Windows

Tip
Double-click on a disk drive icon to display a new window with a directory display from that disk drive.

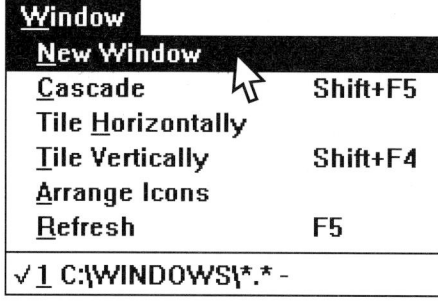

Tip
Click on the appropriate directory window to make it current, or if you cannot see all windows, choose Cascade or Tile option from the menu - this works in the same way as for group/program windows.

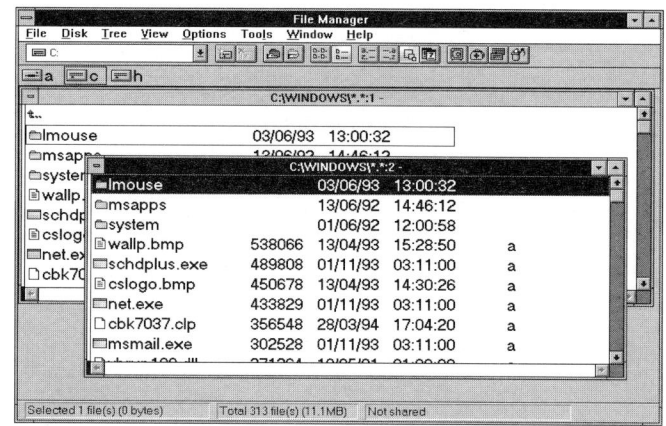

1. Click on the **W**indow menu.

Tip
Shift+Double-click on a directory from the Tree window to display files from it in a new window.

2. Click on **N**ew Window option to display another window.

Note
The new window will have the same display options, as the previous one. Therefore the sort order, the file information and whether you see just the Tree or just the Directory window, or both, is maintained as for the previous window. You can change these options once the new window is created.

The main purpose of opening multiple directory windows is to easily compare files from different directories or disk drives and to copy or move files easily (see later).

Changing the Screen Font

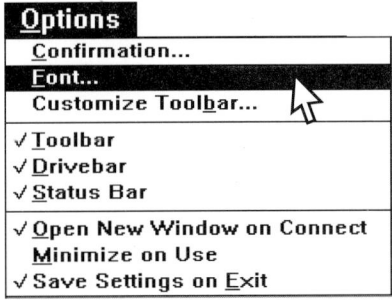

1. Click on the **O**ptions menu.

2. Click on the **F**ont... option to display the Font dialog box.

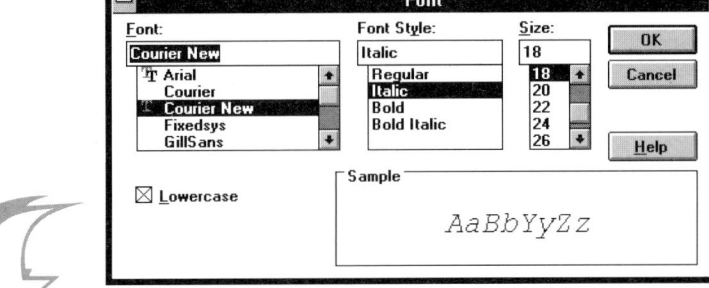

Note

Font names prefixed by TT are called TrueType fonts. These are scalable fonts that print exactly as you see them on your screen.

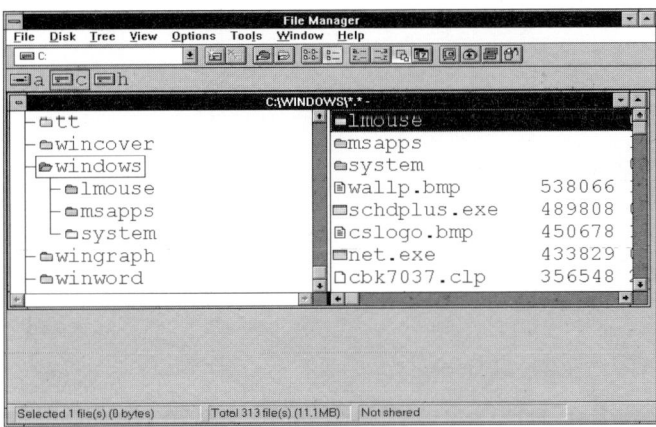

3. Click on the desired **F**ont, Font St**y**le and **S**ize. A sample of the font will be displayed. If satisfied, click on OK.

Changing Disk Drives

Note
Make sure you have inserted a disk into a floppy drive before selecting it.

1. Click on the required disk drive icon. The directory of the drive chosen will then be displayed.

Note
If your system has other additional drives, their drive icons will automatically be displayed. e.g. 'b' for the second floppy disk drive.

An outline around a disk drive icon means that it is the currently selected drive.

Changing Directories

Shortcut
For changing the directory -
***Up/Down cursor** for one directory above or below*
***Page Up/Down** for a directory, one window above or below*
***Home** for the root directory*
***End** for the last directory*
***First letter of a directory name** changes to that directory.*

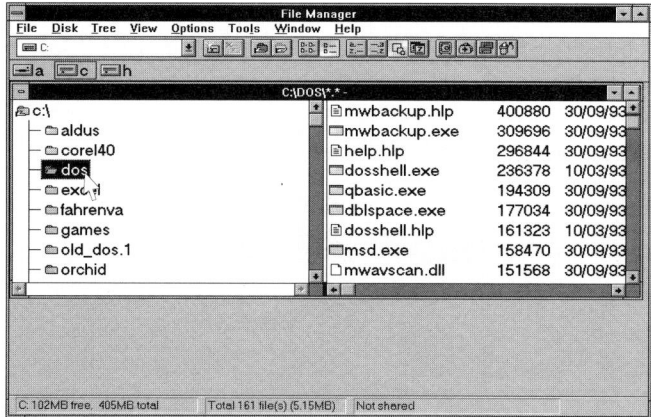

1. Click on the directory folder to change to it. The selected directory will be highlighted and sub-directories (if any) as well as files from it will be displayed.

Expanding Directory Branches

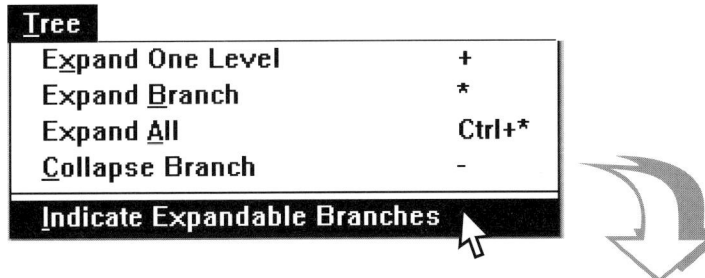

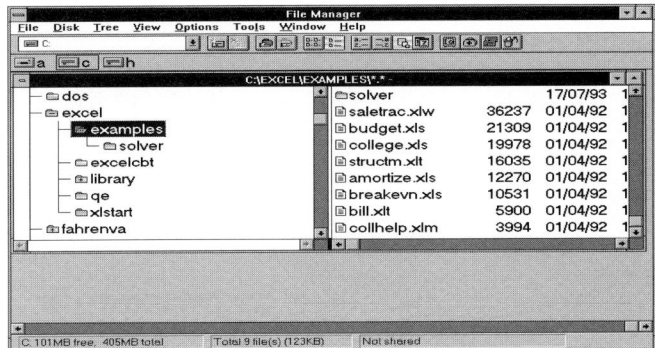

1. Click on the **T**ree menu.

2. Click on the **I**ndicate Expandable Branches option. This will then show a '+' sign in the directory folder if it contains any subdirectories and a '-' sign if a directory is already expanded. If neither signs are present, then the directory has no subdirectories.

3. Double-click on a directory folder with a '+' sign to expand it to one level or Double-click on a directory folder with a '-' sign to collapse the whole branch.

Note
*You can also click on the relevant options from the **T**ree menu to expand/collapse directory branches.*

Shortcut
Press + to expand one level, - to collapse the whole branch, * to expand the whole branch, Ctrl+* to expand all branches that exist.

Creating New Directories

1. Click on the Create Directory... option from the File menu.

2. Type in the name of the new directory in the dialog box and click on OK.

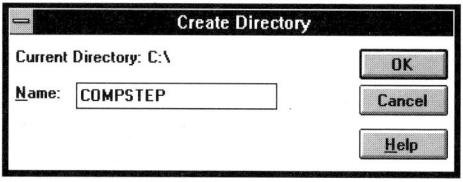

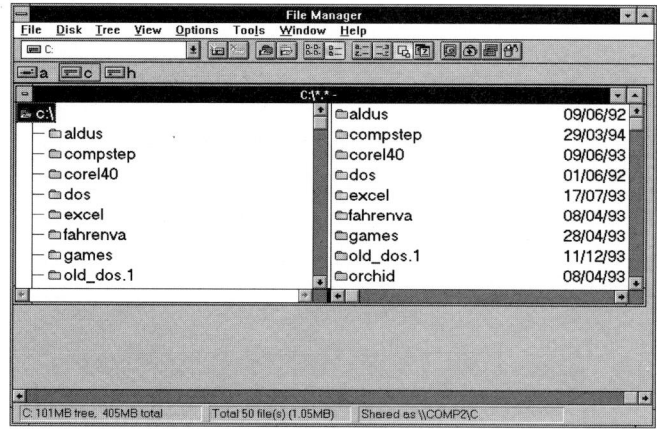

3. The new directory will be created as a sub-directory of the currently highlighted (selected) directory.

Sharing your Directories

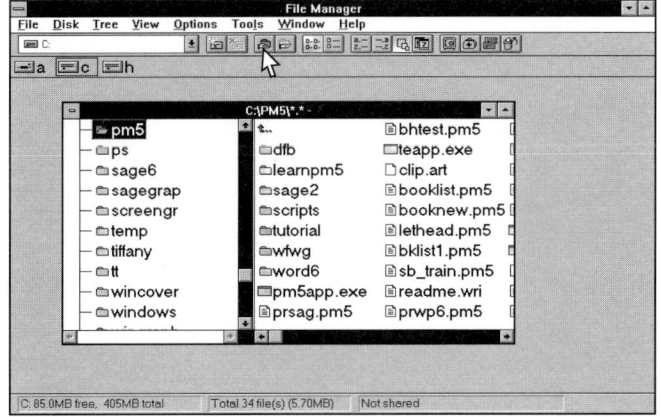

Tip
If someone needs to access the whole of your hard disk, simply share the root (c:\) directory - all sub-directories will automatically be shared.

1. Select the directory to be shared. Click on the Share As button on the Toolbar (or choose Share **A**s... on the **D**isk menu). The Share Directory dialog box will appear.

2. Select Access Type and Password(s) if appropriate, then click on OK. The directory will now appear with a shared directory icon.

Tip
Use the comment to explain what is in the directory.

Note
By default, everyone connected to the network will have **R**ead-only access to all the files in the directory you are sharing - type a R**e**ad-Only Password to restrict access to only users you give the password to. If others need to update your files then check the **F**ull option and again you can restrict access by typing a Fu**l**l Access Password. To allow some users Read-Only and others Update access, check on **D**epends on Password and type two different passwords. Then give the appropriate password to the relevant users.

Unsharing your Directories

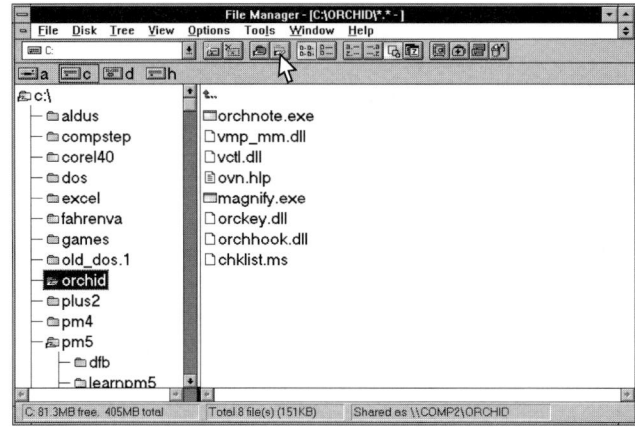

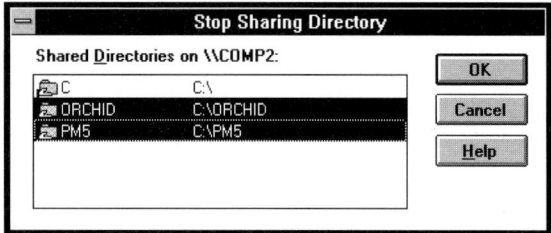

1. Click on the Stop Sharing button on the Toolbar (or select Stop Sharing... from the **D**isk menu). The Stop Sharing Directory dialog box then appears.

2. Select the Directory you wish to stop sharing and click on OK. The Shared Directory icon will be removed from the Directory.

Note
If anyone is using the directory when you stop sharing it, they may lose data and therefore you will be prompted to confirm your action.

Connecting to a Shared Directory

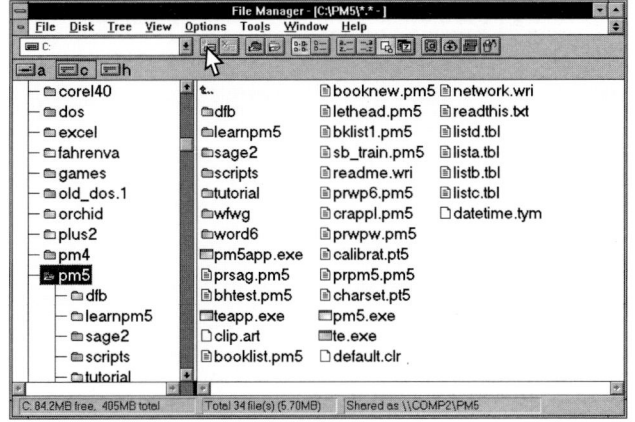

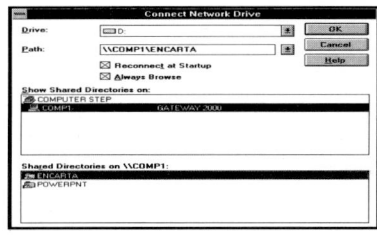
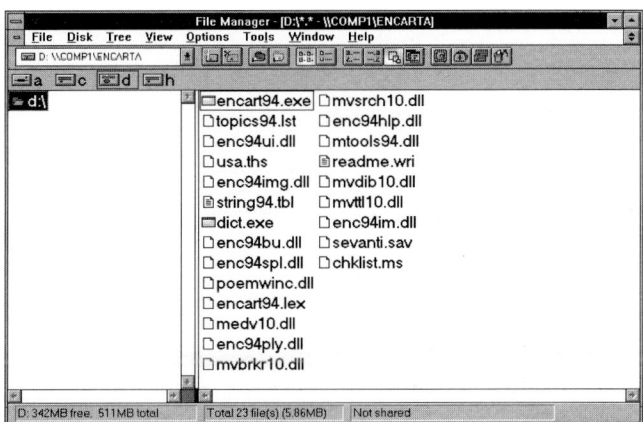

Tip

If you regularly need to connect to shared directories, check on Reconnect at Startup and also ensure that the user giving you shared access has Re-share at Startup checked from the Share Directory dialog box. Now providing both machines have WFWG running you have an automatic sharing capability and connection.

Tip
Click on pull-down arrow and choose from a previously-used path to save typing it again.

1. Click on the Connect Network Drive Button (or select Connect Network Drive.. from the Disk menu). The Connect Network Drive dialog box will then be displayed.

2. Choose the Drive letter or leave the default setting, which will be the next letter in sequence.

3. Type the Path of the directory including the computer name or simply type the computer name and select from the list of shared directories displayed at the bottom.

4. Click on OK and you will be connected to the chosen directory.

Note
Computer name in a path should be preceeded by \\. For example, \\COMP2\WINWORD\CUST.

Tip
You can also double-click on the Workgroup name to display computers that the workgroup consists of. Then select one computer from this list to display it's shared directories at the bottom and then select the required shared directory to connect to it.

Chapter 3. Managing your Files

Seeing who is using your Directories

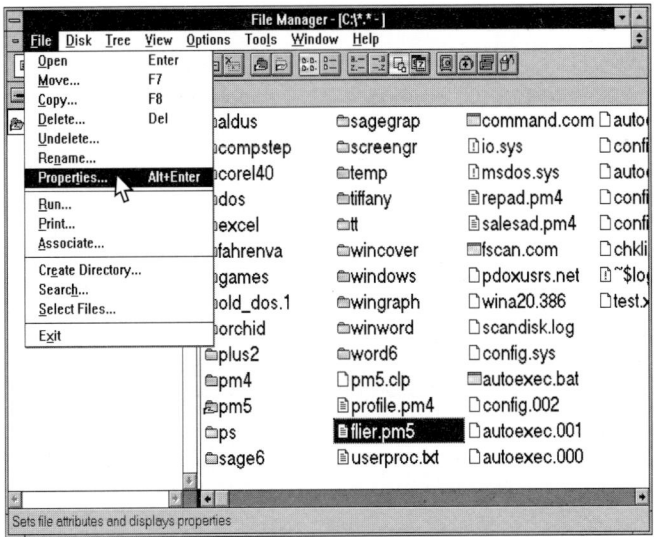

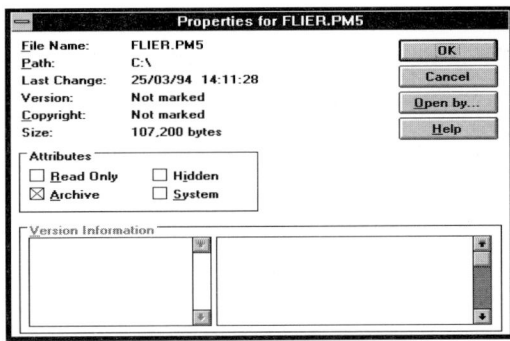

Tip
You can also find out who has access to your files and directories from the Netwatcher facility in the Network Program Group.

1. Select the Directory or File you are interested in and choose Proper_t_ies... from the _F_ile menu. The Properties dialog box will appear.

2. Choose _O_pen By... from the dialog box. The Network Properties dialog box will appear which will show you who is using your directory or files and will indicate the type of access that they have.

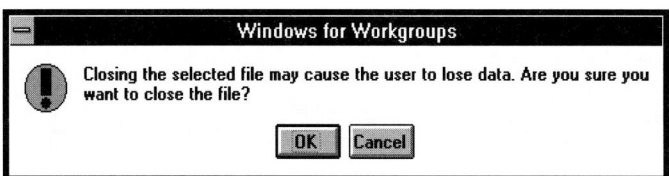

3. If you wish to close a file or directory which someone is using, select it and click on the C_l_ose Files button. A warning box will appear asking you to confirm that you want to close the files. Click on the OK button.

Disconnecting from a Shared Directory

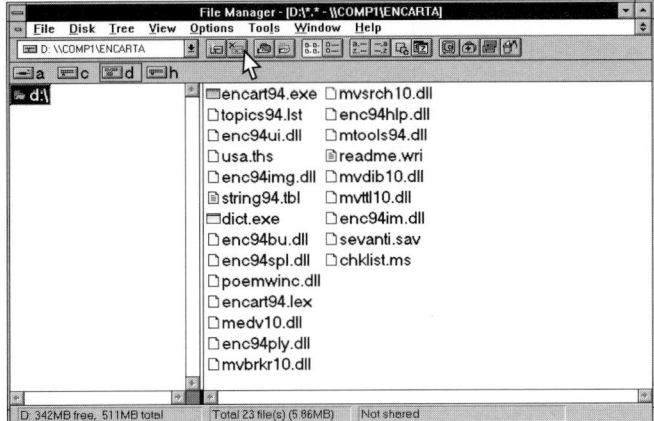

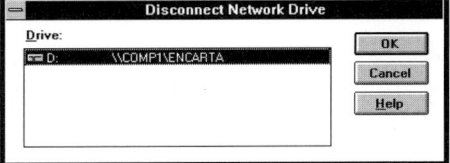
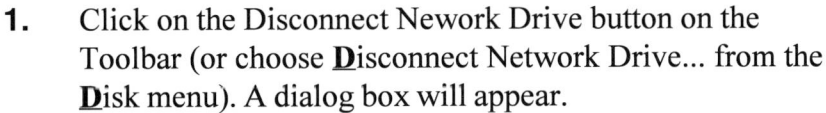

1. Click on the Disconnect Nework Drive button on the Toolbar (or choose **D**isconnect Network Drive... from the **D**isk menu). A dialog box will appear.

2. Click on the desired directory and choose OK. You will then be disconnected from the selected network drive.

Selecting Files

Note
Before you can move, copy, rename or delete files, you need to select them.

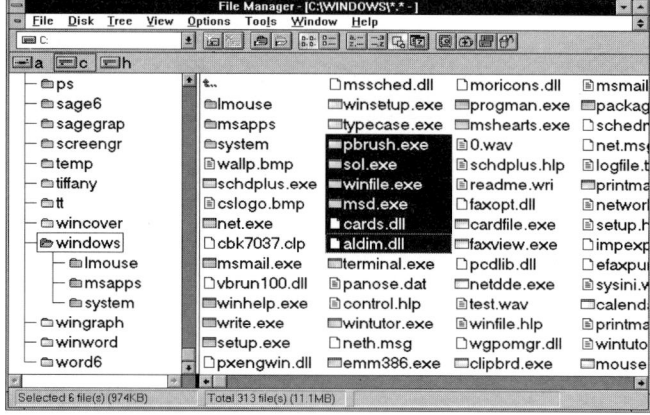

1. Click on any file to select it. The file will be highlighted when selected.

Shortcut
To select all files, press Ctrl+/.

2. To select several adjacent files, click on the first file and then press and hold down the Shift key. Then click on the last file. The whole block of files will be highlighted.

Tip
To deselect all files - adjacent or non-adjacent, click on any one file once.

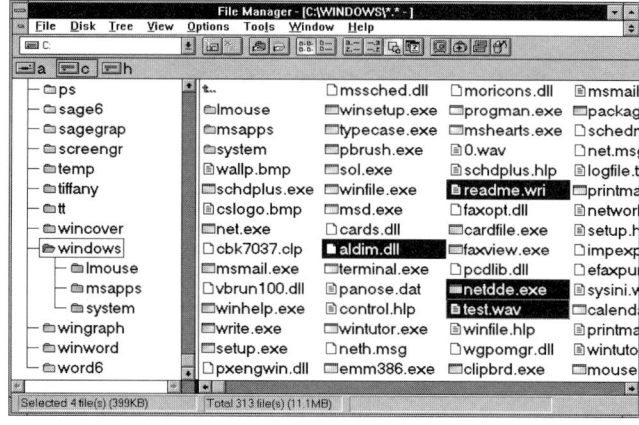

Tip
If you select a file by mistake, Ctrl+click on it again to deselect it.

1. To select several non-adjacent files, press and hold down the Ctrl key. Then click on as many files as required.

Chapter 3. Managing your Files

1. Click on the **F**ile menu.

2. Click on the **S**elect Files... option to display the Select Files dialog box.

Note

Use this technique of selecting more than one file if part of the name is the same.

3. The dialog box can be moved, like any window, so that most of the file names in the current directory are visible.

4. Type in a selection in the File(s) box. For example, ?a*.*, where ? and * are wildcards. A ? represents any one character in that position and a * represents any number of characters.

5. Click on the **S**elect button. The files selected will then be outlined.

Copying/Moving Files or Directories

Note
Use this method to make another copy of a file within the same directory, or another copy of the whole directory at the same level.

Shortcut
F8

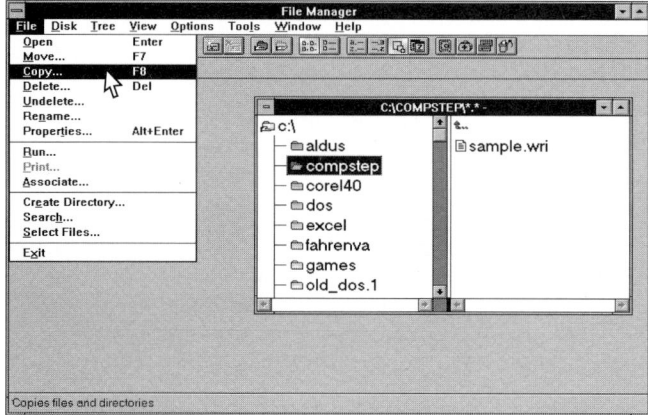

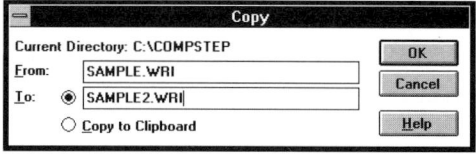

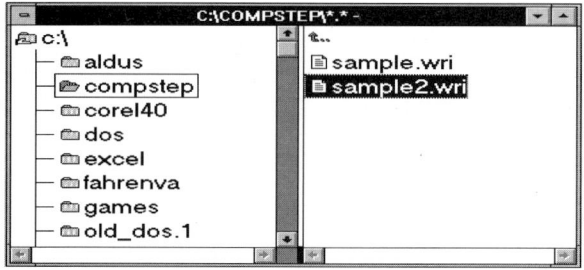

Note
To move files or directories choose Move... from the File menu instead of Copy...

1. Click on a file or directory to select it for copying.

2. Click on the the **C**opy... option from the **F**ile menu to display the Copy dialog box.

3. Type in the new file or directory name.

4. Click on the OK button.

Chapter 3. Managing your Files

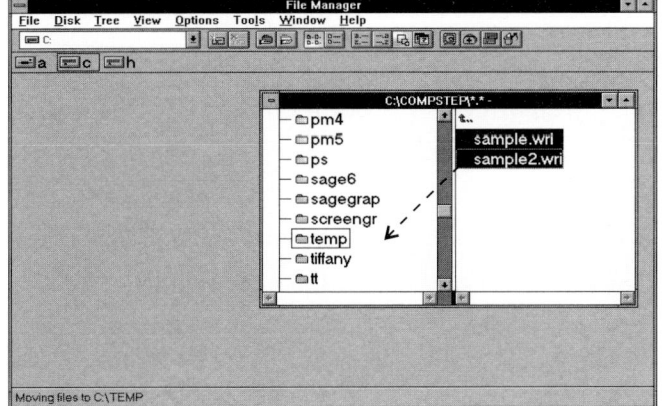

Note
Use this method to move files or directories within the same disk drive.

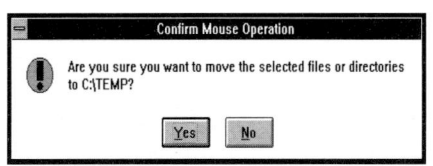

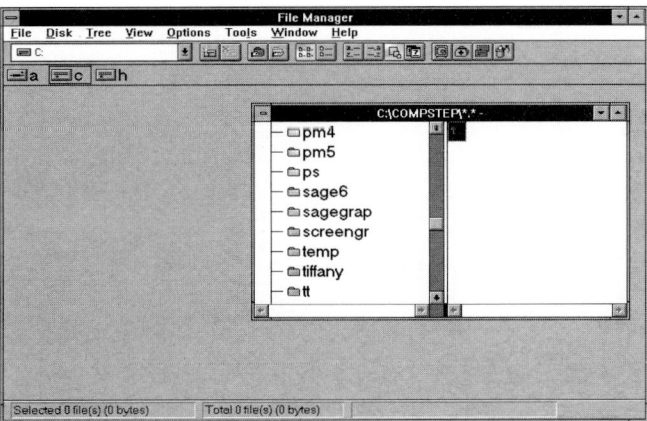

1. Select one or more files to be moved (see Selecting Files) or Click on a directory to be moved (if the selected directory has other sub-directories, they will all be moved).

Note

To Copy files instead of moving them, press the Ctrl key whilst dragging the mouse.

2. Drag the mouse towards the directory you want to move the files into or the directory under.

3. When the required directory is outlined, release the mouse button. A dialog box asking you to confirm the move will be displayed.

4. Click on the **Y**es button. The selected files will then be moved to the chosen directory, or the selected directory group will be re-established under the chosen directory.

Note

Use this method to copy files to another disk. It is particularly useful for backing up selected files onto floppy disks.

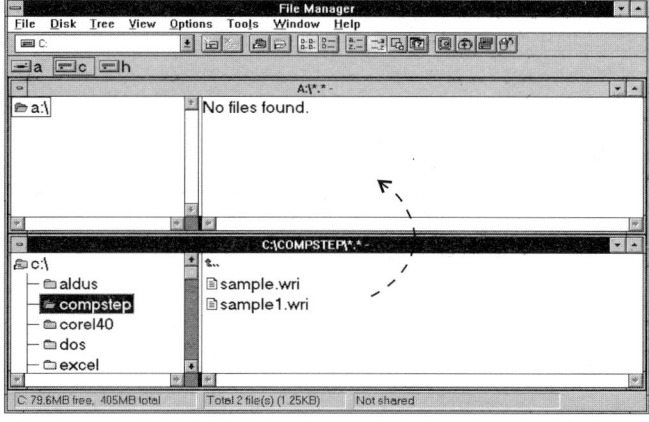

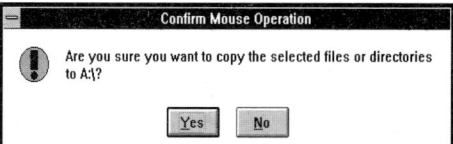

1. Open a new window, select the drive you want to copy files onto and then **T**ile the source and destination drive windows as shown. If you are not sure how to achieve all this, refer to the Working with Multiple Windows section.

2. Select files/directory to be copied.

Chapter 3. Managing your Files

3. Drag the mouse from the selected files/directory to the destination drive window.

4. Release the mouse button when the pointer is in the destination area. A dialog box asking you to confirm the copy will be displayed.

5. Click on the **Y**es button. The selected files/directories will then be copied one at a time.

Note
To Move files/ directories instead of copying them, press the Shift key whilst dragging the mouse.

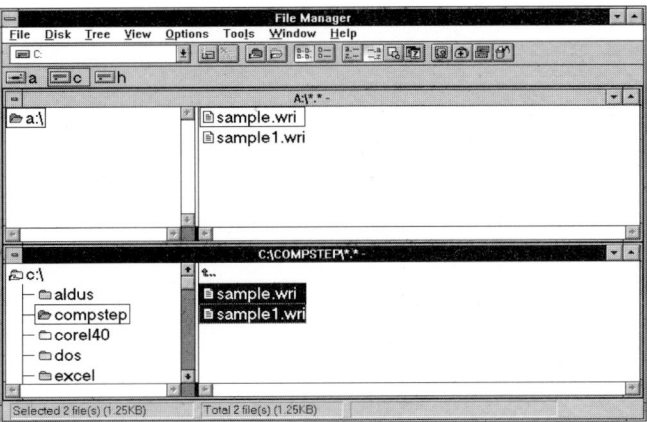

Tip
You can also Copy/Move files or directories to another disk by simply dragging them to the appropriate disk drive icon near the top - it will be outlined if selected!

Summary

Drag-and-Drop using the Mouse	Operation	Key to Press	Icon displayed
To same Disk	MOVE		□
	COPY	CRTL	⊞
To another Disk	MOVE	SHIFT or ALT	□
	COPY		⊞

Deleting Files or Directories

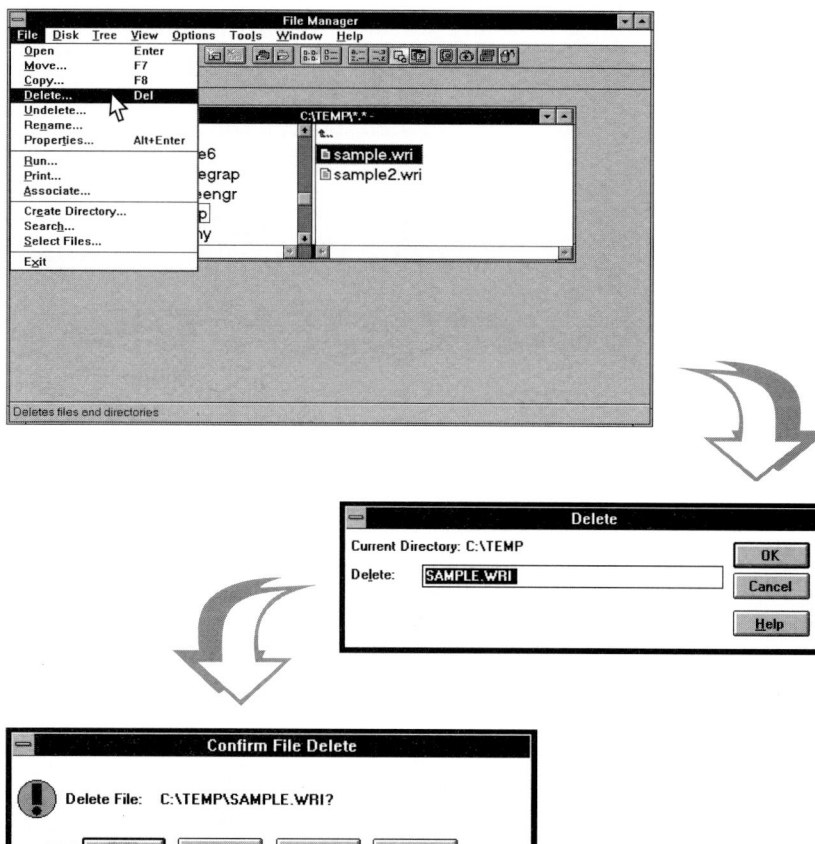

1. Click on a file or directory to delete or select several files to delete at the same time.

Shortcut
Press the Del key.

2. Click on the **D**elete... option from the **F**ile menu to display the Delete dialog box.

3. Click on the OK button if the correct files are displayed in the Delete dialog box. Another dialog box to confirm deletion is then displayed.

4. Click on the '**Y**es' button to delete a file/directory at a time or 'Yes to **A**ll' button to delete all at the same time.

Undeleting Files or Directories

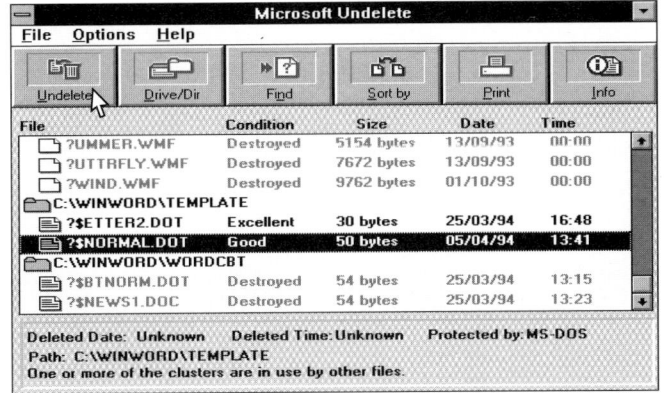
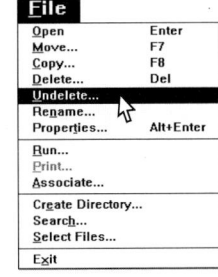

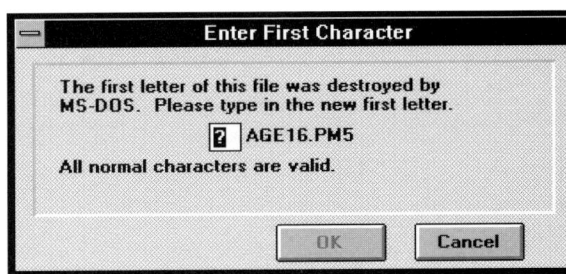

Tip
If you delete a file or directory, the sooner you try to undelete it the more likely it is that it can be recovered.

Warning
Undelete may not always be able to recover a file or directory as it may have been overwritten.

1. Click on the Run Microsoft Undelete button (or select Undelete... from the File menu) on the Toolbar. The Microsoft Undelete screen then appears.

2. Click on the Drive/Dir button and the Change Drive & Directory dialog box appears.

3. Highlight the drive or directory you want to look at. Click on OK and a list of deleted files and directories in the selected drive or directory will be shown.

Tip

If you want a copy of the list of deleted files and directories, click on the Print button, which will print out a list using the default printer.

OR

3. Click on the Find button on the Toolbar. The Find Deleted Files dialog box will be displayed. Type the name of the file you want to find in the Files Specification box and click on OK. The files are then displayed in the Microsoft Undelete screen.

Note

The condition of the deleted files and directories will be described as being Perfect, Excellent, Good, Poor and Destroyed. Files which are described as Poor or Destroyed cannot be recovered. Those described as Good may have been partly overwritten and so may not be recoverable. Files which are described as Perfect or Excellent should be recoverable.

Tip

If you want more information about a directory or file, select it and click on the Info button.

4. If you want to sort the files, click on the Sort by button and the Sort by dialog box will be displayed. This lists six Sort by criteria; Name, Extension, Size, Deleted date and time, Modified date and time and Condition. Click on the option you want and then click on OK. The list of deleted files and directories will now be displayed in the sorted form.

Tip

Although the file has been recovered, it may not be completely intact, so you should check to see whether it has been corrupted.

5. Select the file you want to recover and click on Undelete. A dialog box then appears prompting you to enter the first letter of the file name (which was removed when the file was deleted). Enter a letter and click on OK. The file will now be described on the Microsoft Undelete screen as Recovered.

Note

When a file is deleted, it is not physically removed from your disk - it's just tagged as being deleted by removing its identifying code so that the space it occupies can be re-used. The more file operations that occur after a file has been deleted, the more likely it is that it will have been overwritten.

Renaming Files or Directories

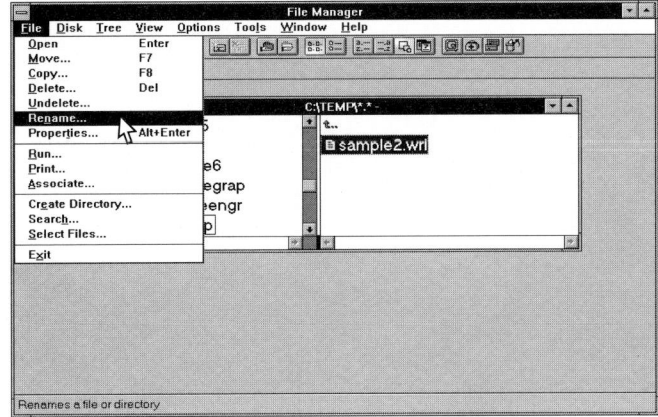

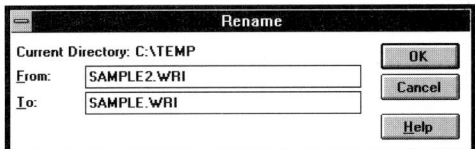

1. Click on a file or directory to rename.

2. Click on the Rename... option from the File menu to display the Rename dialog box.

   Shortcut
   Alt+F,N

3. The selected file/directory name will be displayed as the 'From:' entry. Type in the new file/directory name in the 'To:' box.

4. Click on OK. The selected file/directory will then be renamed to the new name.

Note
You cannot rename a file to a name that already exists in the same directory or a directory to a name that already exists at the same level.

Searching for Files

Shortcut
Alt+F,H

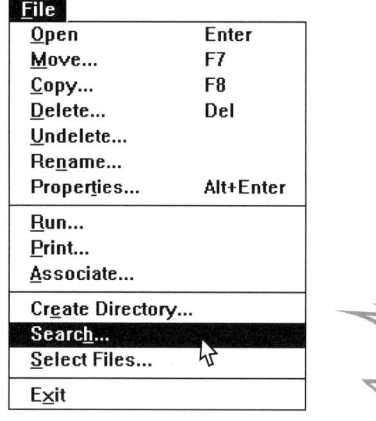

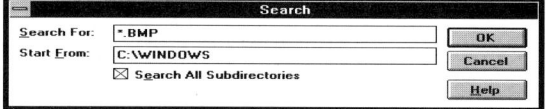

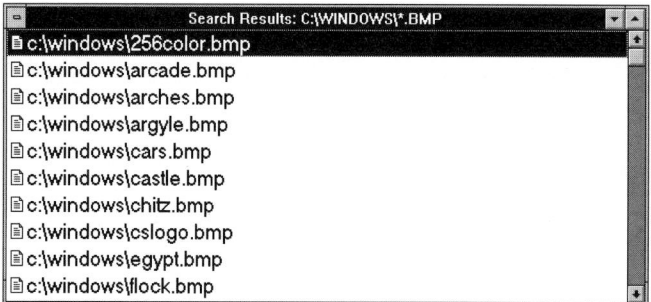

Tip
If you know that the file is in the selected directory, deselect 'Search All Subdirectries' by clicking on its check box - the X will disappear. The search will then be faster.

Tip
You can move or copy files from the Search Results window into other directories or drives.

1. Click on Search option within the File menu.

2. In the Search dialog box, either type in the exact file name you want to find, or use wildcards (* and ?) to find a number of files meeting the search criteria.

3. Click on OK. If the files are found, their names will be displayed in a new window together with path names.

Changing File Attributes

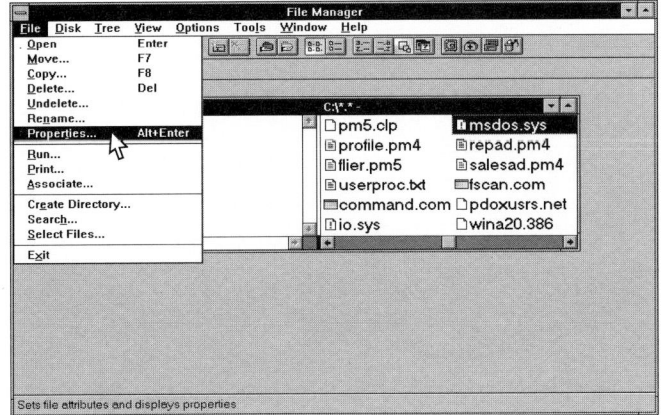

Tip
Select several files, as described under Selecting Files, to change file attributes of all of them at the same time.

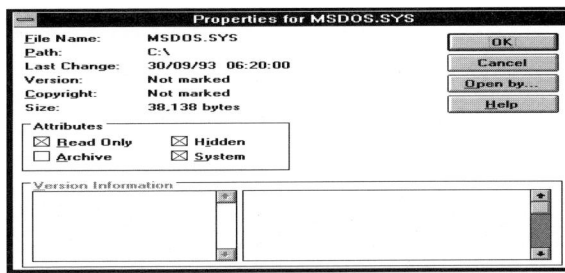

Tip
To select any Hidden/System files, display them first by choosing the option, By File Type... under the View menu and click on the box for Show Hidden/System Files.

1. Select a file by clicking on it.

2. Click on Properties... from the File menu. The Properties dialog box will then be displayed.

3. There are four attributes a file can have. If there is a cross-hair in the box in front of an attribute, then that attribute is set on. Click on it to set it off. If there isn't a cross-hair, click inside the little box to set the attribute on.

4. Click on OK to accept the changes made.

Note
The four attributes are: R (Read Only) - cannot change a file. A (Archive) - indicates if a file has changed since the last backup. H (Hidden) - file does not appear in the directory listing. S (System) - indicates that a file is an MS-DOS system file.

Associating Files to Applications

Tip
The benefit of associating files to applications is that you can double-click on a file from the File Manager and the application will run automatically, opening the file at the same time.

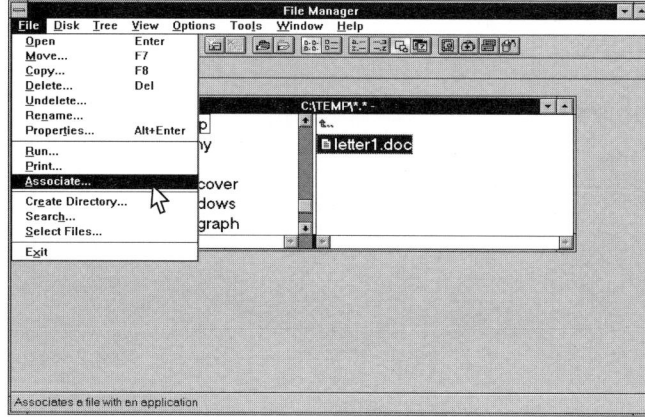

Note
*Many applications are already associated with standard file types when installed. e.g. **Paintbrush** uses **BMP** (bit-mapped graphic), **PCX** and **MSP**. **Cardfile** uses **CRD**, **Clipboard** uses **CLP**, **Calendar** uses **CAL**, **Write** uses **WRI**, **Word** uses **DOC**, **Excel** uses **XLS**, **Lotus** uses **WKS**. However, to create your own association follow these steps.*

1. Select a file by clicking on it.

2. Click on **A**ssociate... from the **F**ile menu. The Associate dialog box will then be displayed listing the programs in the current directory.

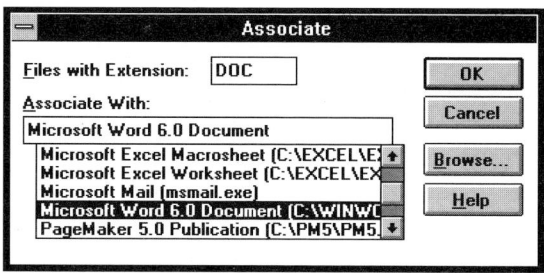

3. Click on the scroll arrows to find an appropriate program to associate the file with. If you cannot find one, click on the **B**rowse button to search through programs in other directories.

4. When the correct program is found, click on it to select it.

5. Click on OK. The selected file will then have a document-file icon next to it, indicating that it is associated with a program. Now you can start the application and open the document from File Manager by simply double-clicking on the file.

Starting Applications from Files

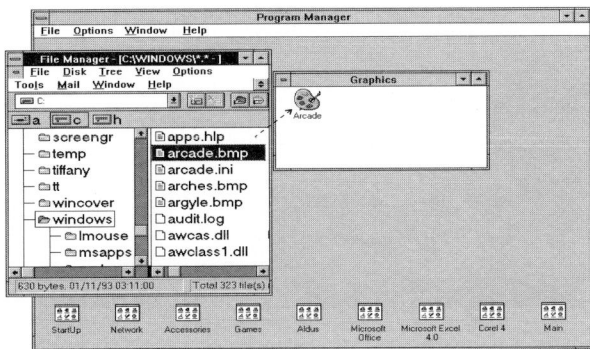

1. Create a new group window as described in Chapter 2.

2. Start File Manager and resize its window as well as the new group window so that they both appear on the desktop at the same time.

3. Select a document file and drag it to the group window. The icon for the program associated with the file will appear automatically and the file name will be displayed under it.

4. Double-click the program icon at any time to start the application and load the associated file at the same time.

OR

1. Double-click a program file to start a particular program. A program file has a file extension of COM, EXE, PIF or BAT.

OR

1. Drag a file to a program file to start the program and open the dragged file at the same time.

Formatting a Disk

Note
Formatting prepares a new disk for use, so that information can be copied onto it.

Tip
You should not format a disk to a higher capacity than it is designed for.

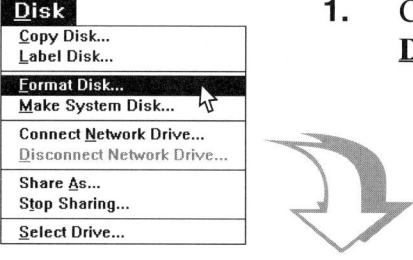

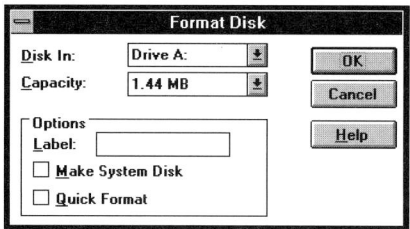

1. Click on **F**ormat Disk... from the **D**isk menu.

2. In the Format Disk dialog box, click on the Down-arrows relating to '**D**isk In' and '**C**apacity' to reveal possible options. Click on the drive that the disk is to be formatted in and to the correct capacity respectively.

3. Click on OK. A confirmation dialog box will then appear. If you click on Yes, formatting will commence.

Warning
Formatting a disk destroys any information that may already exist on it.

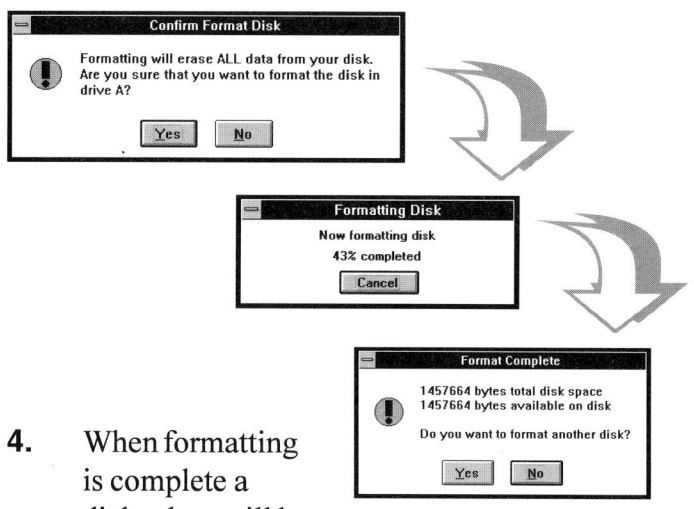

4. When formatting is complete a dialog box will be displayed asking if you want to format another disk.

Labelling a Disk

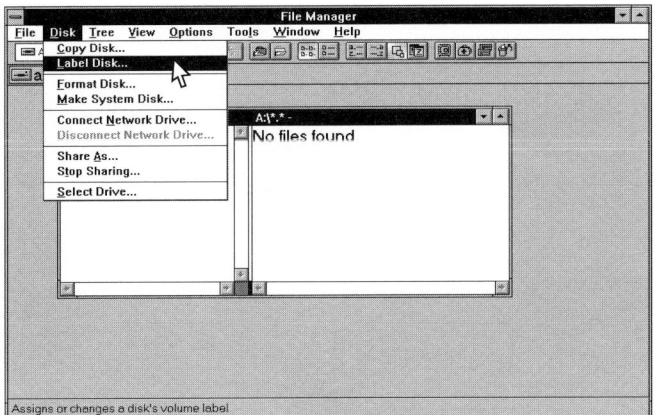

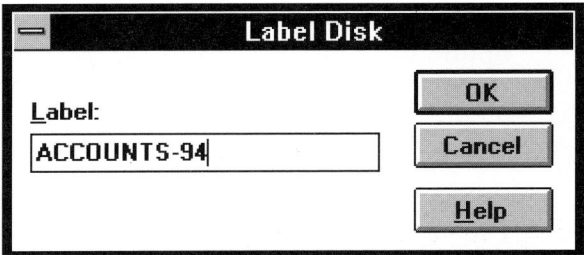

Note
A disk label helps to identify the contents of a disk.

1. Click on the appropriate disk drive icon for the disk you want to label.

2. Click on **L**abel Disk... from the **D**isk menu. Its dialog box will then be displayed.

3. Type in the label (11 characters maximum).

4. Click on OK. The disk will either be labelled for the first time or the old disk label will be replaced by the new.

Note
You also have the option to label the disk when it is being formatted.

Copying a Disk

Note
You can copy a whole disk to another provided both are the same size and capacity.

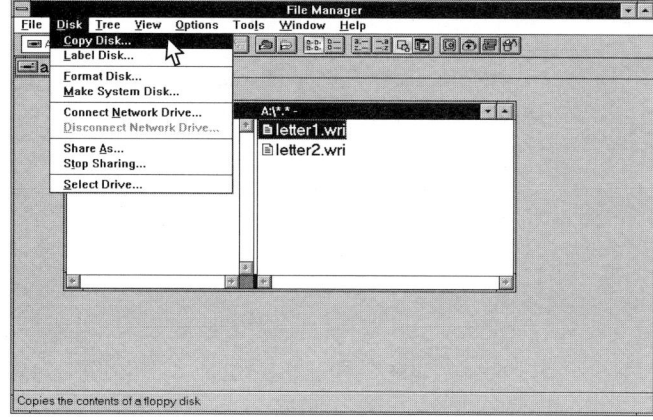

1. Click on the **C**opy Disk... option from the **D**isk menu.

2. You will be asked to select Source and Destination drives if your system has more than one drive. In our example, there is only one drive (a), so the Confirm dialog box is displayed straight away.

Note
If the destination disk is new and not formatted, it will be formatted automatically.

3. Click on OK.

4. Insert the source disk when prompted and click on OK.

5. In a one drive system, once the contents of the source disk are copied, you will be prompted to insert the destination disk. Remove the source disk from the drive first and then insert the destination disk and click on OK.

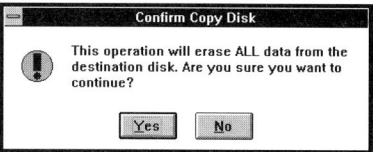

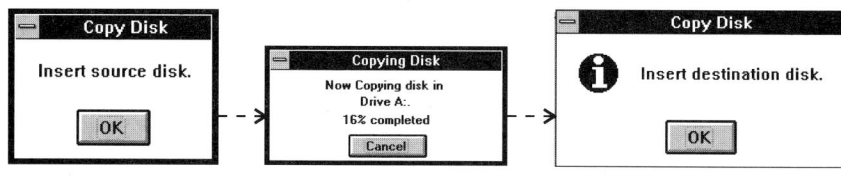

Scanning for Viruses

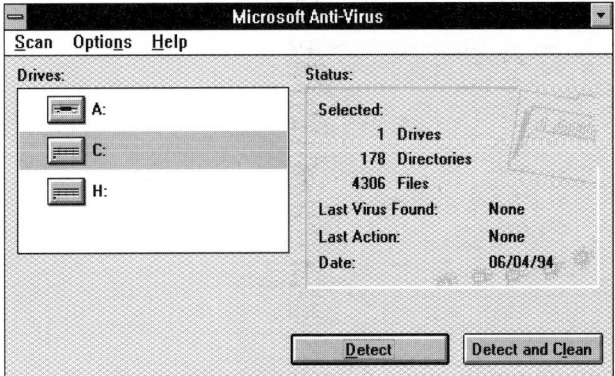

Tip
A virus is a piece of software that can cause severe destruction to important information on your computer - it can spread particularly easily when your computer is in a workgroup.

1. Click on the Run Microsoft Anti-Virus button (or select Antivirus... from the Tools menu) on the Toolbar. The Microsoft Anti-Virus screen then appears.

2. Click on the icon for the drive you want to check for viruses. Then click on Detect to locate any viruses or Detect and Clean if you want to locate and automatically remove any viruses found. If you chose Detect and Anti-Virus detects a virus it will display a dialog box which lets you choose to remove the virus, ignore it, stop the scan or delete the file where the virus has been found.

3. When the scan for viruses is finished, a screen showing the scan statistics will be displayed. Click on OK to return to the Microsoft Anti-Virus main screen.

4. Select Exit Anti-Virus from the Scan menu to exit.

Note
If the File Manager Toolbar does not show the Run Microsoft Anti-Virus button, it can be added by selecting Customize Toolbar... from the Options menu.

Backing up your Hard Disk

Tip
Backing up your hard disk regularly is a good safeguard against losing all your data should you have a hard disk fault.

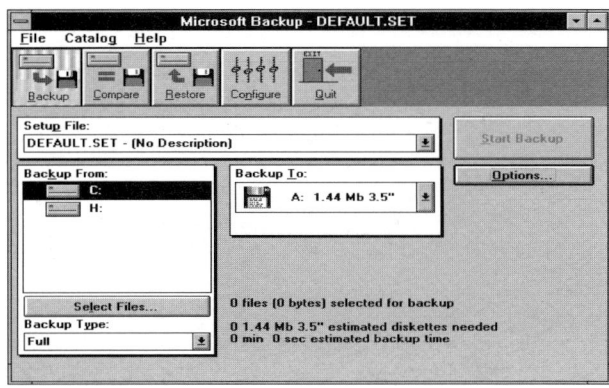

Note
The first time you use Backup, you will need to select Configure which will do a small test backup/compare to ensure compatibility.

1. Click on the Run Microsoft Backup button (or select Backup... from the Tools menu) on the File Manager Toolbar to display the Microsoft Backup screen.

Tip
If you don't want to back up the whole of your hard disk, click on the Select Files button and choose the files you want to back up.

2. To make a copy of your hard disk files onto floppy disks, double-click on the drive you want to back up and then click on the Start Backup button. The Backup progress screen is then displayed, which tells you when to insert your floppy disks and monitors the progress of the backup.

Note
To Restore a backed up version of your files, click on the Restore button to display the Restore screen. Double-click on the drive or drives to be restored and then click on the Start Restore button. The Restore Progress screen will be displayed, which tells you when to insert your floppy disks and monitors the progress of the restoration.

Note
To Compare your files against a backed up copy, click on the Compare button to display the Compare screen. Double-click on the drive or drives to be compared and then click on the Start Compare button. The Compare Progress screen will be displayed, which tells you when to insert your floppy disks and monitors the progress of the comparison.

CHAPTER 4

Printing

This Chapter Covers

- **Accessing Printers**
- **Installing a Printer**
- **Setting up a Printer**
- **Installing Fonts**
- **Printing from Applications**
- **Using Drag and Drop Printing**
- **Using the Print Manager**
- **Controlling Printing**
- **Using Separator Pages**
- **Sharing your Printer**
- **Unsharing your Printer**
- **Connecting to a Network Printer**
- **Disconnecting from a Network Printer**

in easy steps

Chapter 4. Printing

Accessing Printers

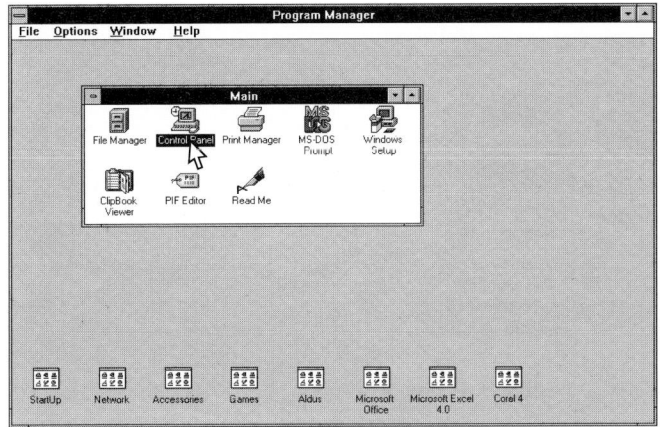

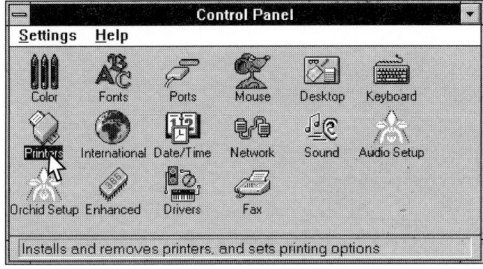

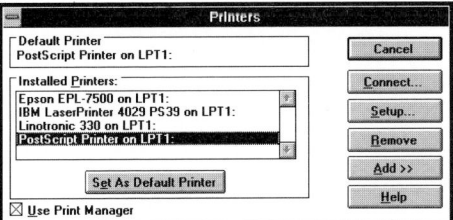

1. Double-click on the Control Panel icon in the Main group.

2. Double-click on the Printers icon from the Control Panel. The Printers dialog box will then be displayed, showing all installed printers.

Installing a Printer

Tip
If your printer is not in the List of Printers, select 'Install Unlisted or Updated Printer' from the list and then insert the disk provided by the printer vendor containing the printer driver.

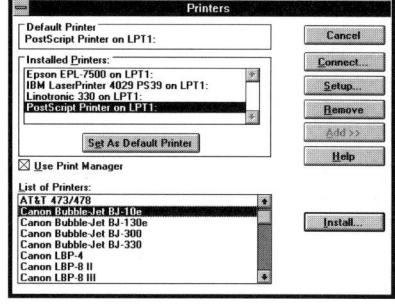

Note
Click on the Connect... button to connect your printer to a printer port from a list. The default is LPT1. Click on the Remove button to un-install the printer.

Note
If you want to use your newly-installed printer from Windows programs, click on the Set As Default Printer after highlighting it.

1. Click on the Add button to display a list of printers at the bottom of the Printers dialog box.

2. Scroll through the list of printers by clicking on the Up/Down arrows until you find your printer.

3. Click on that printer name. It will be highlighted.

4. Click on the Install button. The Install Driver box appears.

5. Insert the requested WFWG master disk. Click on OK. Your printer will appear in the Installed Printers list.

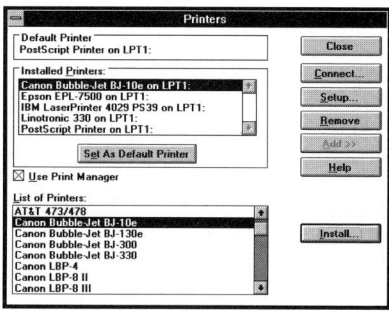

Setting up a Printer

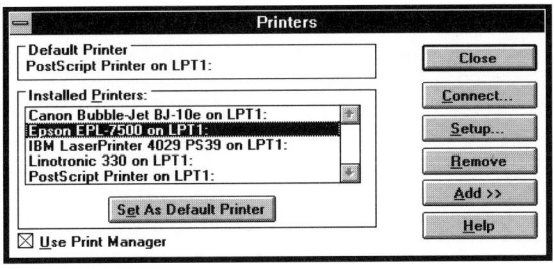

Note
Printers can also be set up in Print Manager by selecting Printer Setup... from the Options menu.

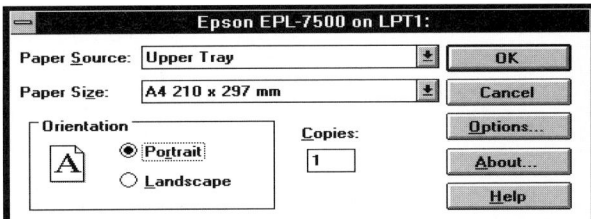

Tip
Click on the Landscape option to print sideways. e.g when printing on envelopes.

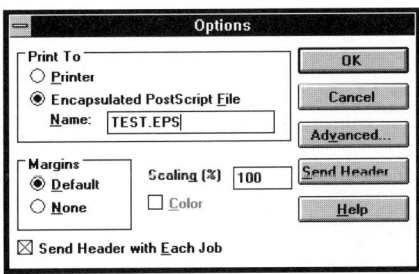

1. Click on the Setup button from the Printers dialog box. A box with the name of your printer in the title bar is displayed.

Tip
To produce high quality output, click on the Advanced... button to set the printer resolution (or dots per inch) and halftone frequency (lines per inch).

2. Click on the down-arrows to reveal a list for Paper Source (e.g. Upper/Lower trays etc.) or Paper size (A4, A5, Legal, etc.). Click on the required settings.

3. Click on the Options button to print to an EPS file. This file can only be printed properly on a PostScript printer.

Tip
Select FILE: instead of LPT1 when you connect the printer to redirect output to a file instead of a printer.

Installing Fonts

Note

Fonts are used to describe different Type faces. Standard fonts are installed automatically when you install Windows for Workgroups. You can install additional fonts by following the procedure described here.

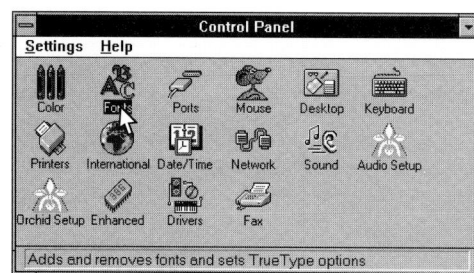

1. Double-click on the Fonts icon from the Control Panel.

2. The Fonts dialog box shows the installed fonts. Click on the **A**dd... button to install additional fonts.

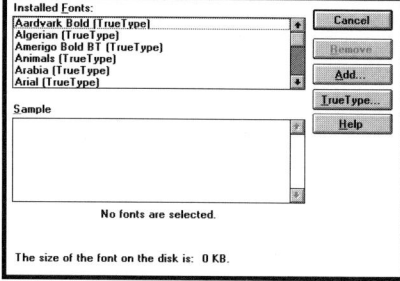

Tip

*Hold down the Ctrl key and click on the font names to select several of them or press the **S**elect All button to install all fonts listed.*

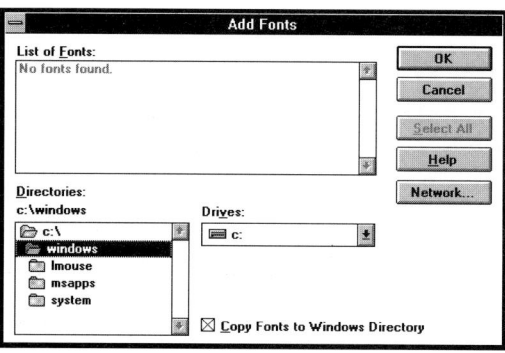

3. Click on the Drive/Directory with fonts. A list will be displayed on screen. Select and click on the OK button.

Chapter 4. Printing

Printing from Applications

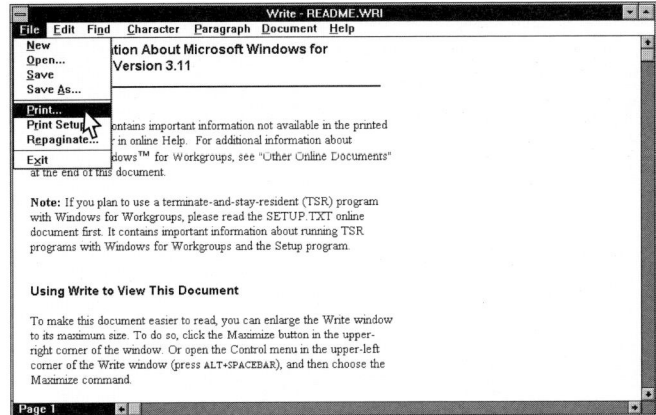

Note
Click on the Setup... button to perform the same functions as already described under Setting Up the Printer.

1. Load any Windows application. e.g. Windows Write.

2. Open a file you want to print from the application or create a new file.

3. Click on the Print... option from the File menu.

4. Click on the Pages option if you only want to print selected pages from the file. Then click on the From/To boxes and type the range of pages you want to print.

5. Click on the OK button.

Using Drag and Drop Printing

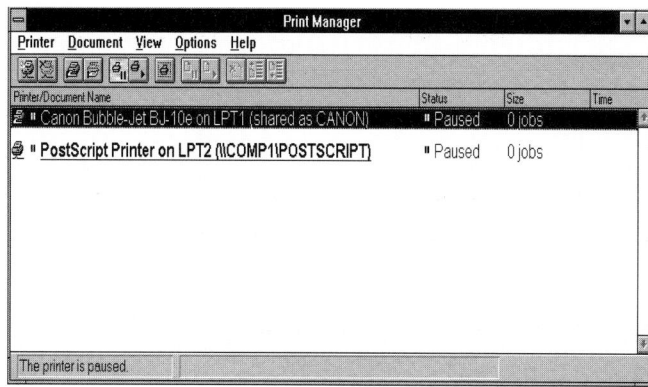

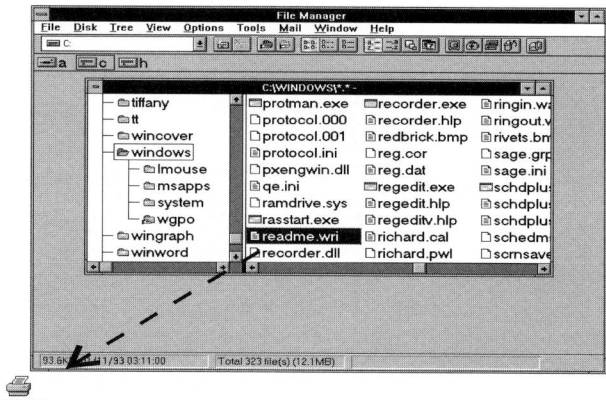

1. Double-click on the Print Manager icon. The Print Manager window will be displayed.

2. Click on the Minimise button to reduce Print Manager to an icon at the bottom of your desktop.

3. Double-click on the File Manager icon to start it.

4. Resize File Manager window so that the Print Manager icon at the bottom is still visible.

Chapter 4. Printing

5. Select the directory from which you want to print a file.

6. Click on the file to print and drag it on top of the Print Manager icon.

7. The file will be opened automatically and so too will the Print box on top of it. Click on OK to print the file.

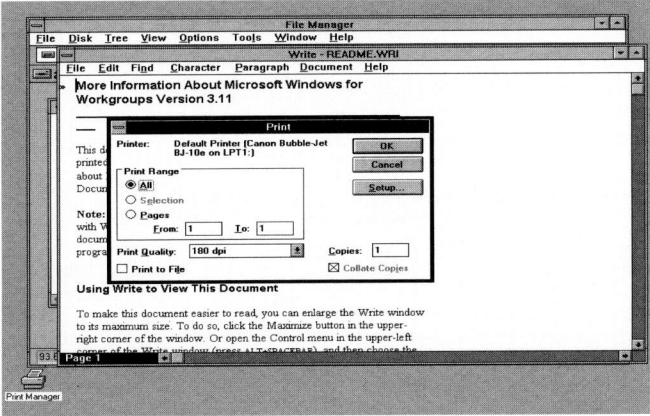

Tip
Use this method of printing if you want to print several files - simply drag and drop them one at a time onto the Print Manager icon.

Using the Print Manager

Note
Closing Print Manager will cancel any files that are being printed. If you want to work on something else, minimise the Print Manager window to an icon to free the desktop for your other applications.

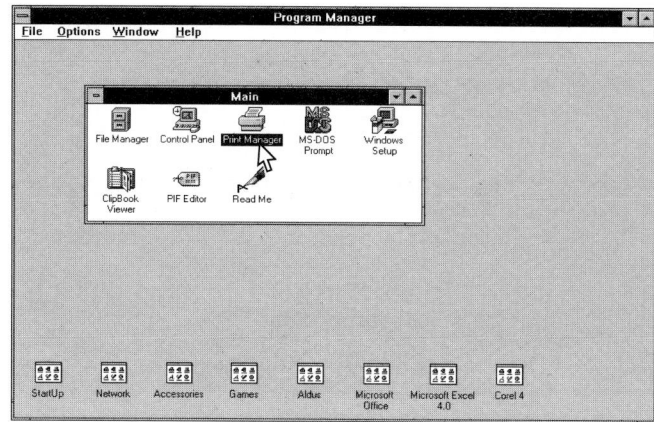

Printer in use
File printing
File in queue
Paused printer

Paused file

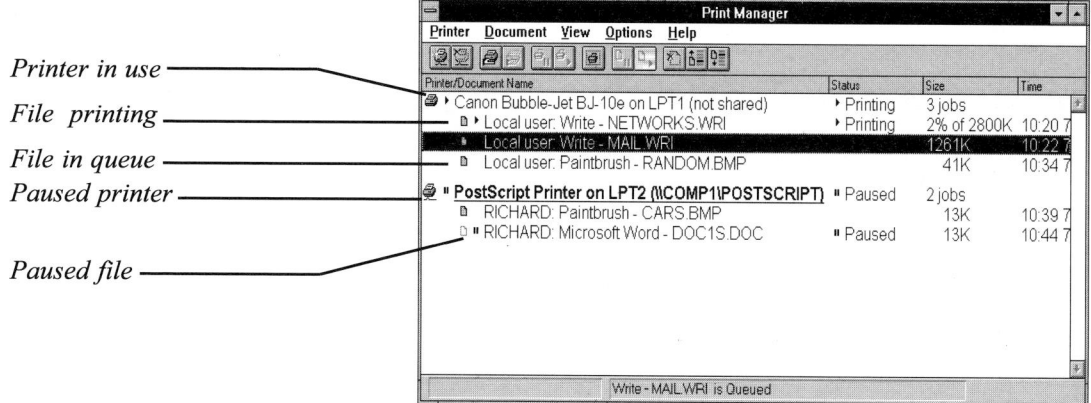

1. Double-click on the Print Manager icon. The Print Manager window will be displayed.

2. When you print a file it will appear in the Print Manager window under the selected printer. The information displayed includes its name, size, percentage of file already printed, date and the time the print job was submitted.

3. Use the Toolbar (or equivalent menu options) to control printing operations.

This button pauses the selected printer. You can't pause a network printer, only your own.

Note
To use these buttons, you must first select the printer or file from Print Manager, by clicking on it to highlight it.

 This button resumes printing on a paused printer.

 This button makes the selected printer into the default printer.

 This button pauses anyone else's files (but not your own) at any time on your own printer. It pauses your own files before they start to print on a network printer.

 This button resumes the printing of a file you have paused.

 This button deletes the selected file. You can delete any files on your own printer, but only your own files on a network printer.

 This button moves the selected file up the print queue. You can only move files on your own printer.

Tip
If you need to re-order documents on a shared printer, use Chat, Mail or WinPopup to ask the owner of the printer to do it for you.

 This button moves the selected file down the print queue. You can only move files on your own printer.

Controlling Printing

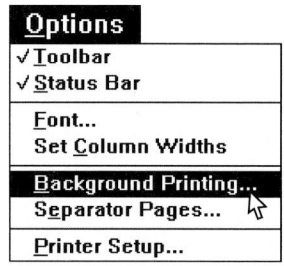

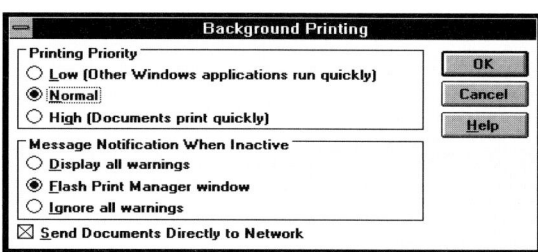

1. To control the speed of your printer, click on the **O**ptions menu in Print Manager and then click on the **B**ackground Printing... option. The Background Printing dialog box then appears.

2. Click on either **L**ow, **N**ormal or Hi**g**h Priority.

Note
Low Priority slows the printer down dramatically but you can perform other work on your computer at virtually the same speed. High Priority allows much faster printing but your other work will slow down as extra memory is reallocated to your printer. Medium Priority is a compromise between the two.

3. Select an option to control what Print Manager should do if any printer problems are encountered. For example, the printer may run out of paper.

Note
Print Manager usually runs as a background activity and therefore this setting is more important. Print Manager can be set to take one of three actions:

Chapter 4. Printing

Alert Always	*Print Manager will display a dialog box with a message describing the problem.*
Flash if Inactive	*The Print Manager icon is displayed on top of other applications you may be using at the time. You will need to double-click on the icon to enlarge Print Manager to a window and investigate further.*
Ignore if Inactive	*Print Manager will ignore the problem. No messages will be given and the print job will be halted.*

Using Separator Pages

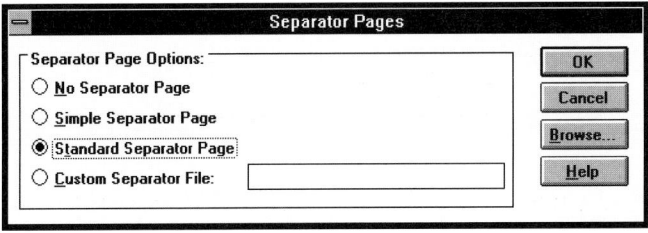

1. Select S**e**parator Pages... from the **O**ptions menu. The Separator Pages dialog box will be displayed with the default setting of **N**o Separator Pages.

2. Select **S**imple Separator Pages (for dot matrix, daisy-wheel printers and any printers which don't accept downloaded graphics), S**t**andard Separator Pages (which uses large fonts and should be used for Laser Printers) or **C**ustom Separator Pages and type in the name of the file you want to use as a separator page.

3. Click on OK and your printer will start to use Separator Pages between each print job.

Tip

Separator pages may be useful in identifying your printed job if the Printer is shared between different users.

Note

A Custom Separator Page file must be a Windows metafile (.WMF) or be in Clipboard (.CLP) picture format.

Sharing your Printer

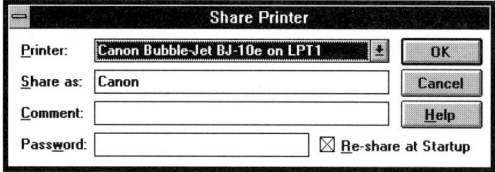

Shared printer icon

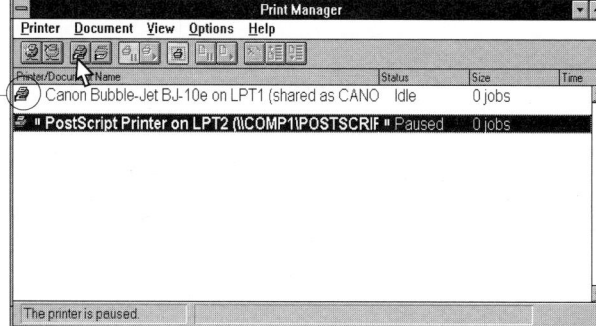

Tip
*If others use your printers regularly, click on the **R**e-share at Startup check box to automatically share the printer each time you log on.*

1. In Print Manager select the printer you want to share and click on the Share As button (or select **S**hare As... from the **P**rinter menu). The Share Printer dialog box then appears.

2. Choose a name for the shared printer, a comment and a password if desired.

Note
The benefit of using a password is to limit the users in your workgroup who can use your printer - only those you give the password to will be able to print on your printer.

3. Click on OK and the printer will appear in the Print Manager screen with a shared printer icon.

Unsharing your Printer

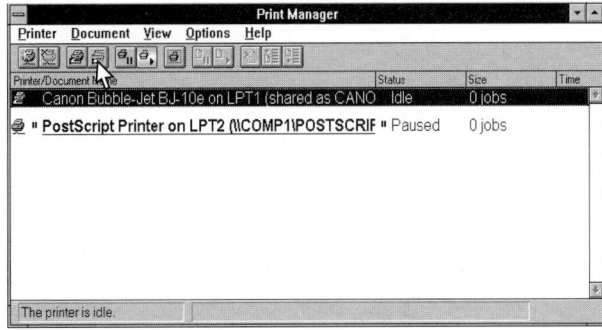

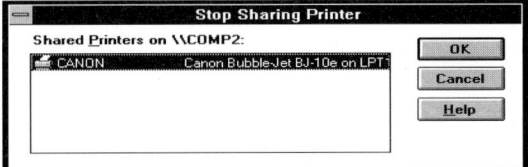

1. Click on the Stop Sharing Printer button on the Toolbar (or select S**t**op Sharing Printers... from the **P**rinter menu). The Stop Sharing Printer dialog box then appears.

2. Select the printer you want to stop sharing.

3. Click on OK and the printer will now be shown on the Print Manager screen with a local printer icon.

Connecting to a Network Printer

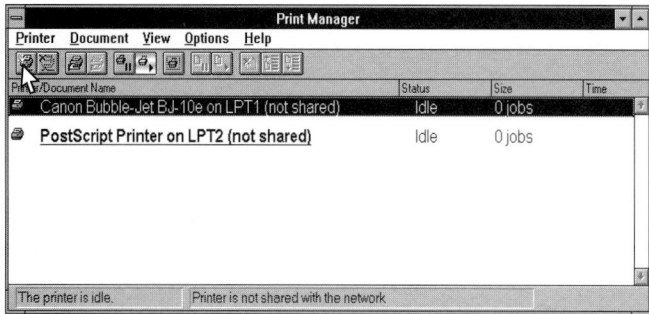

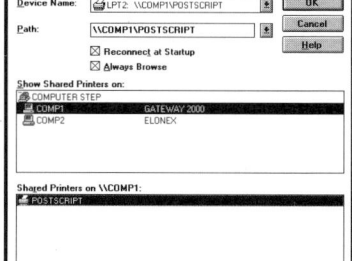

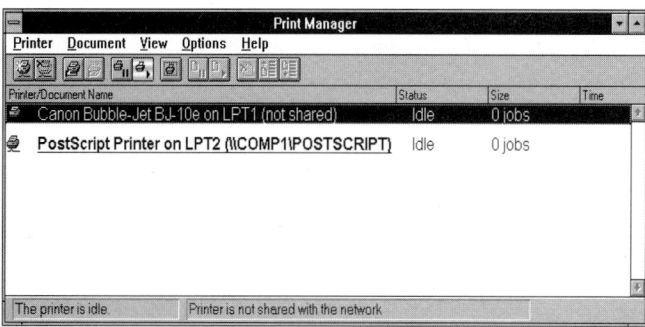

1. Click on the Connect Network Printer button on the Toolbar (or select Connect Network Printer... from the Printer menu). The Connect Network Printer dialog box then appears.

2. Check that the correct **D**evice Port (LPT1, LTP2, etc) is selected for the printer. You need to specify one port for each printer you use including one for each network printer.

Warning
If you use the same device port for local and network printers you will not be able to use both at the same time.

Note
Your computer will have a certain number of device ports physically present (usually one or two), but Windows for Workgroups can set up logical device ports to allow you to print out on network printers. You do not need to possess a physical device port to correspond to each logical device port.

3. Type in the **P**ath for the printer, which will be a double backslash followed by the computer name, then a single backslash followed by the printer's share name. An example of a path is *\\Comp1\Postscript*. Click on a workgroup icon to expand it to show all the workgroup members and click on a computer to show the printers connected to that computer.

Shortcut
Double-click on a printer to connect to it or click on the arrow at the end of the Path box to display a list of the paths you have used recently.

4. Click on the Reconnec**t** at Startup check box if you use the printer regularly, but you will need to ensure that the owner of the printer has checked the **R**eshare at Startup box when they shared the printer. Click on OK and the printer will appear with a network printer icon.

Disconnecting from a Network Printer

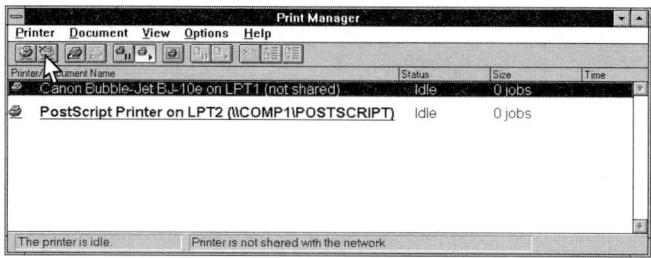

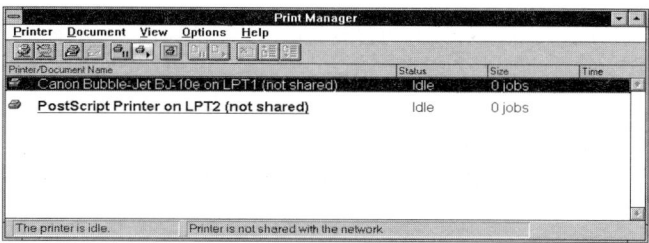

1. Click on the Disconnect Network Printer button on the Toolbar (or select Disconnect Network Printer... from the Printer menu). The Disconnect Network Printer dialog box then appears.

2. Double-click on the printer you want to disconnect or select the printer and click on OK.

Note
When you disconnect from a network printer, it will remain (with an unshared printer icon) on your Print Manager screen, but you will no longer be able to use it.

CHAPTER 5

Customising

THIS CHAPTER COVERS

- Changing the Screen Colours
- Adding a Desktop Pattern
- Adding a Wallpaper
- Using Screen Savers
- Using Fast Alt+Tab Switching
- Changing the Icon Spacing
- Using the Sizing Grid box
- Changing the Cursor Blink Rate
- Customising your Mouse
- Changing the Keyboard Response
- Resetting the Date/Time
- Setting Country-specific Standards
- Using Ports
- Using 386 Enhanced Mode
- Using Sound
- Changing Network Settings
- Cusomising the File Manager Toolbar
- Customising Help

in easy Steps

Chapter 5. Customising

Changing the Screen Colours

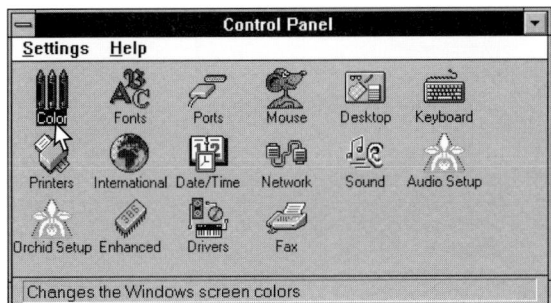

Control Panel

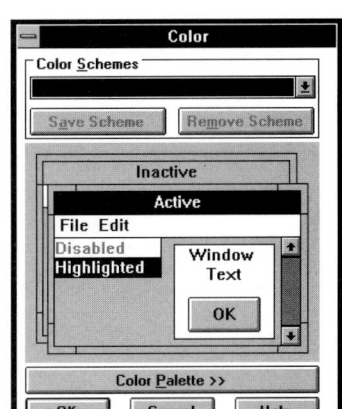

1. Double-click on the Control Panel icon from the Main group to display the Control Panel window.

2. Double-click on the Color icon for the color dialog box.

3. Click on the down arrow under Color Schemes to display a list of standard colour schemes. e.g. Designer, Fluorescent, Monochrome, Pastel, The Blues and so on.

4. Click on the colour scheme you like. The various elements of the screen below will then be displayed in the colour scheme chosen.

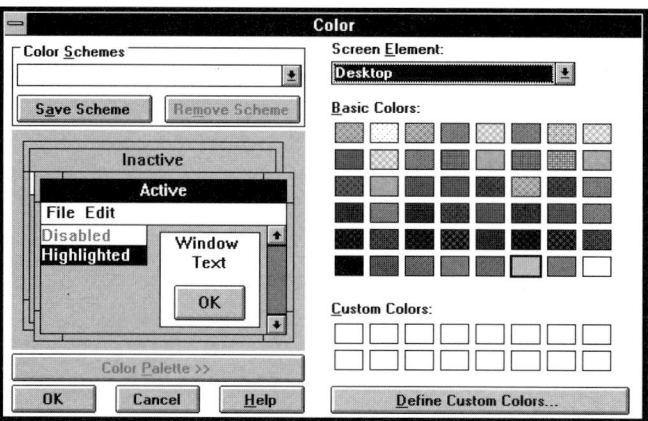

1. Click on the Colour **P**alette button to assign your own colours to various screen elements. A colour palette is displayed on the right.

2. Click on the down arrow under Screen **E**lement to display a list of screen elements. e.g. Desktop, Button Face, Active Border, Scroll Bars, Window text, Highlight.

3. Click on an element you want to change the colour of.

4. Click on one of the 48 basic colour boxes to change the colour of the chosen screen element to that colour.

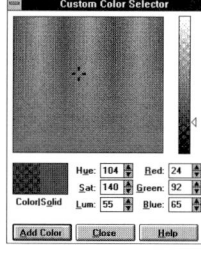

1. Click on **D**efine Custom Colors button to create your own colours. The Custom Color Selector box is displayed.

2. Drag the little cross-hairs on a background of multi-colours in the box. Moving to the right will increase the H**u**e (change of colours) at the bottom. Moving towards the top will increase the **S**at (colour saturation or purity).

3. Drag the little luminosity arrow on the right to adjust the brightness. The **L**um value changes automatically.

4. Click on **A**dd Color to define it as one of 16 custom colours.

Chapter 5. Customising

Adding a Desktop Pattern

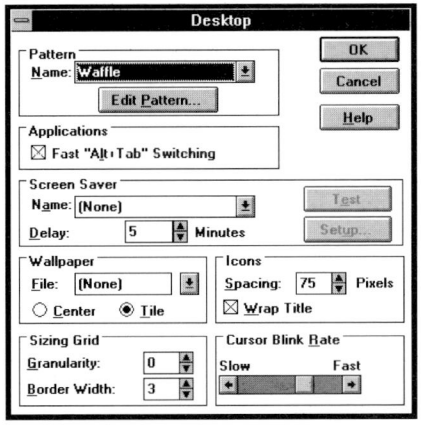

Desktop

Tip
Click on the Edit Pattern... button to create your own patterns from the standard ones supplied.

1. Double-click on the Control Panel icon.

2. Double-click on the Desktop icon from the Control Panel.

3. Click on the down arrow under Pattern to display a list of pattern names.

4. Click on the one that you want. e.g. Waffle.

5. Click on the OK button. The new desktop pattern is displayed.

Adding a Wallpaper

Note
Wallpapers are graphic images that you can use for your desktop instead of patterns.

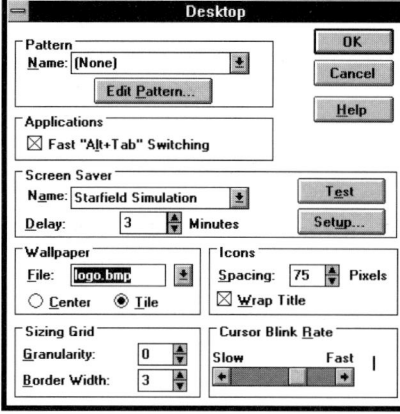

1. Double-click on the Control Panel icon.

2. Double-click on the Desktop icon from the Control Panel.

Tip
You can scan other images to use as wallpapers or create your own wallpapers using Windows Paintbrush. They just need to be saved as BMP (bit-mapped) files.

Note
If you use a Pattern and a Wallpaper, the Wallpaper will be displayed.

3. Click on the down arrow under Wallpaper to display a list of wallpaper file names.

4. Click on the one that you want. e.g. logo.bmp.

5. The Tile option should be clicked. This repeats the wallpaper image across the whole desktop. The Center option only displays one copy of the image in the center.

6. Click on the OK button.

Using Screen Savers

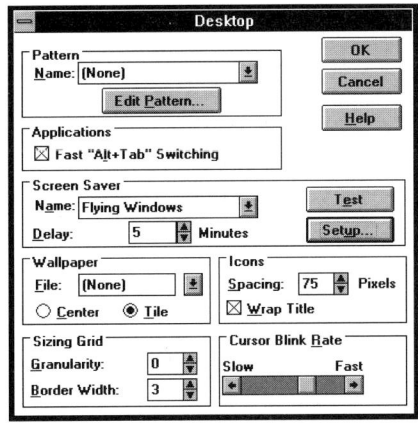

1. From the Desktop box, click on the down arrow under Screen Saver to display a list of them.

2. Click on the one you want to use. e.g. Flying Windows.

Note
Screen Savers are images displayed on the screen if there is no activity for some time. This is supposed to prevent your screen from burn-out.

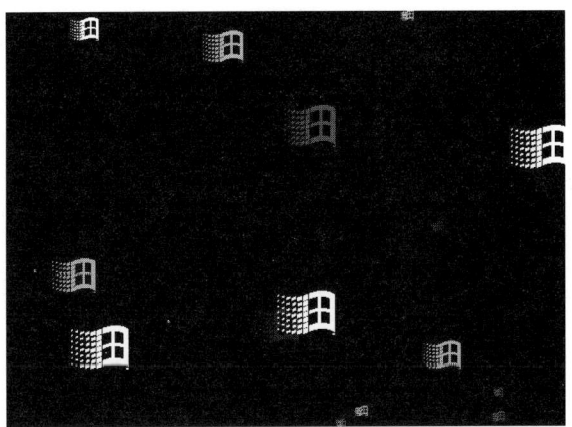

3. Click on the Test button to see the selected screen saver image.

4. Click on the Setup button to customise the screen saver.

5. Click on the up/down-arrow for Delay to control how long the keyboard/mouse is idle before the screen saver starts.

6. Click on the OK button.

Note
Previous sections describe how to access the Desktop box.

Using Fast Alt+Tab Switching

Note
All settings described on this page are made from the Desktop box. To access the Desktop box refer to earlier pages.

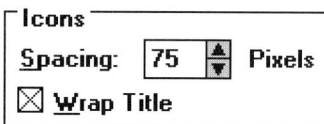

Click on the Fast Alt+Tab Switching box in the Desktop so that a cross appears. This allows you to quickly switch between several applications running by pressing Alt+Tab keys.

Changing the Icon Spacing

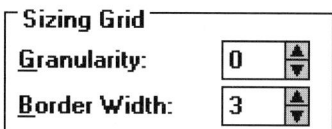

Click on up/down arrows to change the spacing between icons or just type in a new value. Check the **W**rap Title box to ensure that longer icon names are wrapped to the next line instead of being truncated.

Using the Sizing Grid box

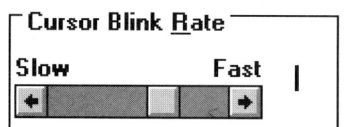

Click on up/down arrows to use **G**ranularity and change the **B**order Width. Granularity is invisible grid lines used to align Icons/Windows. Border Width is the width of window borders.

Changing the Cursor Blink Rate

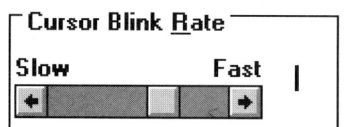

Click on the left/right arrow to decrease or increase the rate at which the cursor blinks on the screen. A small vertical cursor line will blink inside the Cursor Blink **R**ate box so that you can determine the effect of your setting immediately.

Chapter 5. Customising

Customising your Mouse

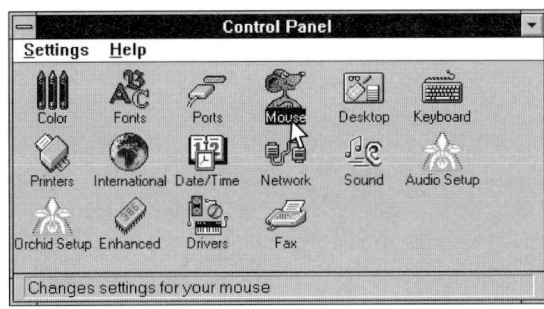

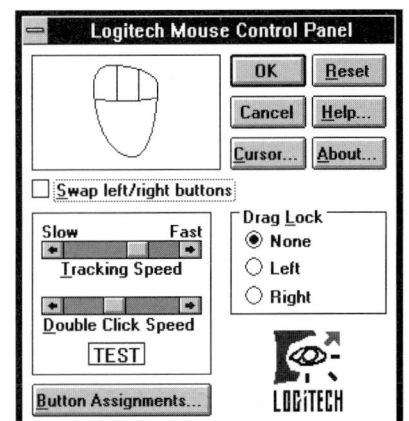

Note
The make of mouse you have attached to your computer may vary and so your mouse icon and Mouse Control Panel may differ from the one shown. However, most Mouse Control Panels will offer the same range of customising options.

1. Double-click on the Mouse icon from the Control Panel. The Mouse Control Panel will then be displayed.

2. Drag the scroll box under the **T**racking Speed towards Fast for a quicker movement of the mouse pointer.

3. Drag the scroll box under **D**ouble Click Speed towards Slow if you prefer windows to recognise a double-click even if you have not clicked the mouse button in very rapid succession. Test the double-clicks on the TEST box. It will be highlighted and un-highlighted when your double-clicks are recognised.

4. If you are left-handed select **S**wap left/right buttons.

5. If you click on **C**ursor... you can customise the appearance and motion of the mouse pointer on the screen.

Note
You can click on the left or right arrow instead of dragging the scroll box.

Changing the Keyboard Response

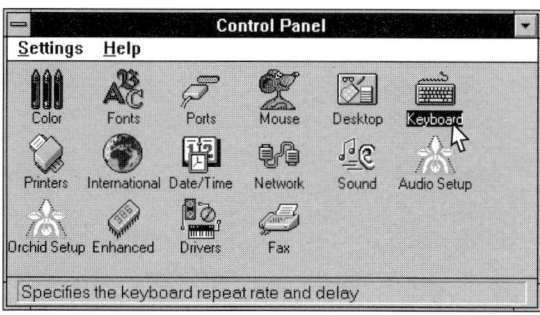

Note
You can click on the left or right arrow instead of dragging the scroll box.

1. Double-click on the Keyboard icon from the Control Panel. The Keyboard dialog box will then be displayed.

2. Drag the scroll box under **R**epeat Rate to control how fast or slow a key repeats itself when you hold it down.

3. Drag the scroll box under **D**elay Before First Repeat to control how long or short a time your computer waits before it starts repeating a key that you have held down.

4. Once you have set the two keyboard speed scroll boxes, click inside the Test box. Then hold a key down to test your settings.

5. Click on the OK button.

Resetting the Date/Time

Note
Your computer has an internal clock which can be reset. Some applications use this clock to determine the current date and time.

1. Double-click on the Date/Time icon from the Control Panel. The Date & Time dialog box will then be displayed.

2. Reset the **D**ate and **T**ime by simply typing them in. Alternatively, click on the up-arrows or down-arrows to increase or decrease the date/time respectively.

3. Click on the OK button.

Note
*See the next section to change the format of the **D**ate or **T**ime to meet specific country requirements. For example, the American date format is month/day/year whereas the British standard is day/month/year.*

Setting Country-specific Standards

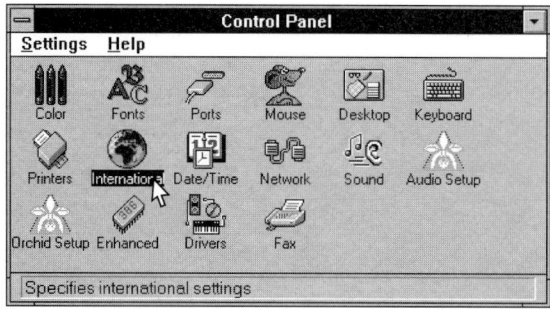

1. Double-click on the International icon from the Control Panel. The International dialog box will then be displayed.

2. Click on the down-arrows to select from a list of Countries, Languages, Keyboard Layouts, and Measurements.

3. The current Date, Time, Currency and Number formats are displayed. Click on the appropriate Change... button to alter the format of any of these.

4. Click on the OK button.

Using Ports

The Ports icon allows you to change settings for the communication ports used by your computer. These are COM1, COM2, COM3 and COM4. Communication ports are used by serial devices e.g. a modem, mouse. Refer to the manual for the particular device to find out the settings that need to be made.

Ports

Using 386 Enhanced

By default WFWG will run in enhanced mode. This allows Non-Windows programs to be run at the same time as Windows ones and allows you to use shared facilities. Sometimes these programs will compete for the same device, like a printer (technical jargon for this is *device contention*). Use this icon to specify how WFWG should deal with this problem and how it should schedule applications running simultaneously.

386 Enhanced

You will also be able to use 32-bit file and disk access from here to improve performance.

Using Sound

If you have installed a sound card, use the Sound icon to associate a particular sound to an event. For example, when WFWG starts, when an information box is displayed or when an error has been made.

Sound

Use the Drivers icon to install various multimedia drivers. A driver is software that controls how a particular device works e.g. CD-ROM, Videodisc player.

Drivers

Changing Network Settings

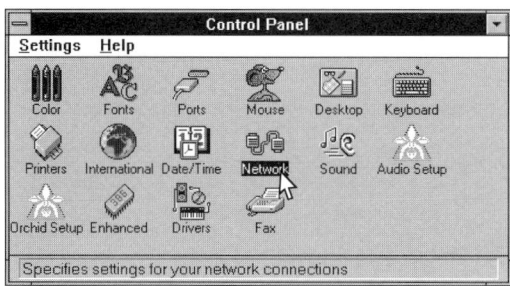

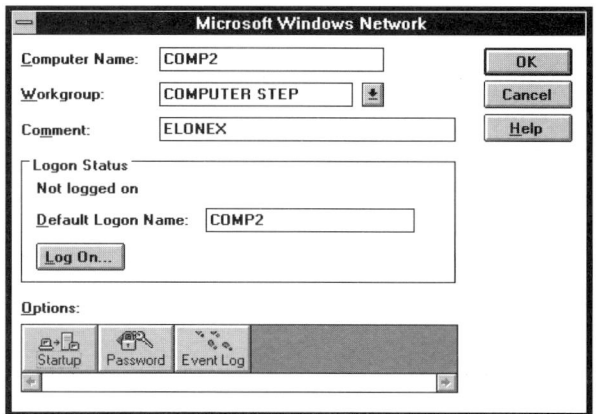

1. Double-click on the Control Panel icon in the Main group. The Control Panel will appear.

2. Double-click on the Network icon. The Microsoft Windows Network screen then appears. This allows you to change some of the basic operations of the network.

3. To change any of your computer's details, click on the appropriate box and type the change.

4. To change your Password click on the Password button and the Change Password dialog box will be displayed. Type in your **O**ld Password and then the **N**ew

Chapter 5. Customising

Password, which you will need to repeat in the Confirm New Password box.

5. To use the event log, click on the Event Log button and select the events that you want to record.

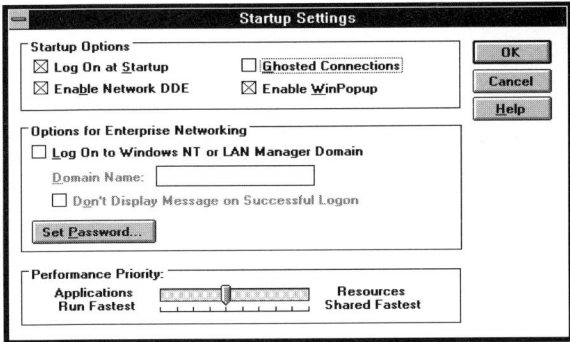

6. To change the start-up settings, click on the Startup button.

7. Choose the Startup options you want using the check boxes. Log On at Startup should be checked if you want to use shared facilities regularly. Enable Network DDE should be checked if you use Chat, Clipbook viewer or other network applications. Ghosted Connections reserves a drive letter for each network connection rather than establishing the connection at startup. Enable WinPopup automatically starts WinPopup when you Log on.

8. To make your own applications run faster, use the mouse to drag the Performance Priority slider to the left. To make resources you are sharing with others run faster, drag it to the right.

Tip
If selected, the Ghosted Connections setting can speed up your startup.

Customising the File Manager Toolbar

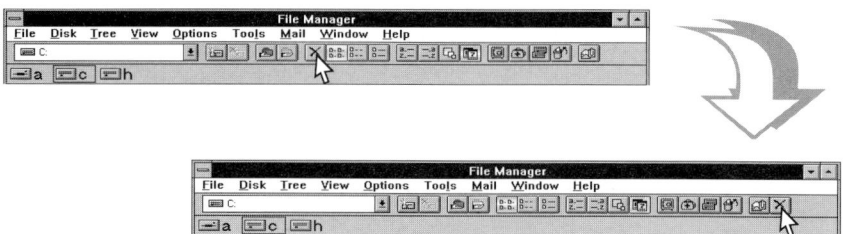

1. To move buttons along the Toolbar, press Shift and drag the button to the place you want it. You can drag a button a short distance to create a space.

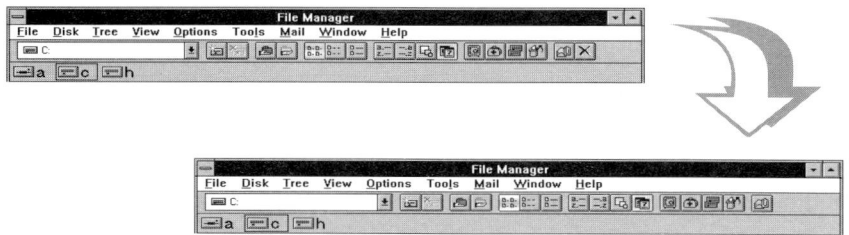

1. To remove a button from the Toolbar, press Shift and drag the button off the Toolbar.

Note
*Buttons which you remove in this way are not lost permanently and can be put back by selecting Customize Tool*b*ar... from the* **O***ptions menu.*

1. In File Manager, select Customize Tool**b**ar... from the **O**ptions menu or double-click on the Toolbar background. The Customize Toolbar dialog box then appears.

Chapter 5. Customising

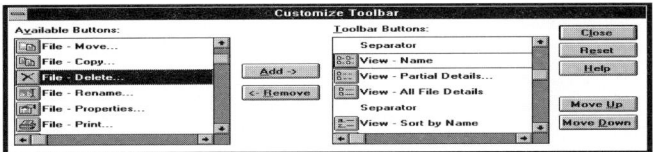

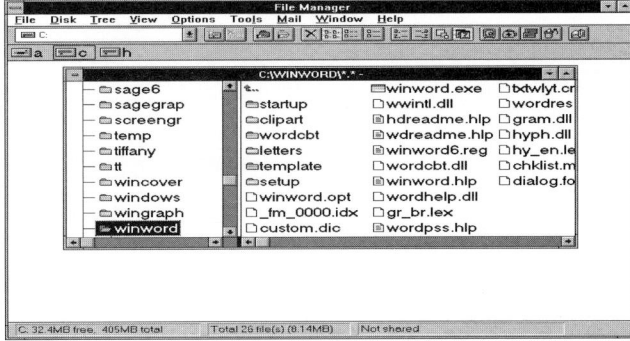

Tip
Drag the dialog box out of the way so you can see your changes as you make them.

Warning
Once you get into the Customize Toolbar dialog box and make changes, you must undo each change individually if you change your mind or Reset to the default arrangement.

2. To add a button to the Toolbar select it from the A**v**ailable Buttons box and click on the **A**dd button. You can create spaces between buttons by adding Separators.

3. To remove a button from the Toolbar, select it and click on the **R**emove button.

Tip
Remove buttons you don't use very often to free up space for the ones you use a lot.

4. To alter the order of the buttons, select the one you want to move in the **T**oolbar Buttons box and click on Move **U**p (to move it to the left on the Toolbar) or Move **D**own (to move it to the right).

Note
*If you want to return to the default button arrangement, click on R**e**set.*

5. When you have finished your customising, click on the C**l**ose button to exit from the Customize Toolbar dialog box.

Customising Help

Note
You can customise WFWG Help. See Chapter 1 to learn how to use Help.

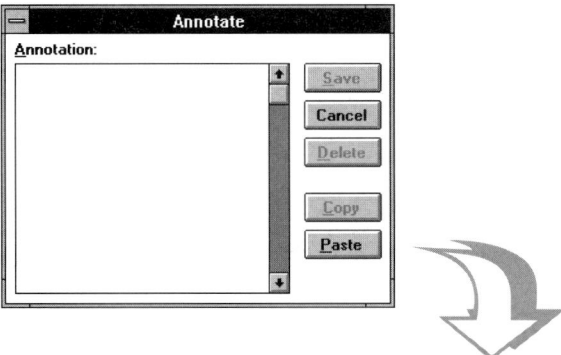

Paper clip symbol indicates that this WFWG Help text is annotated.

1. Click on **E**dit menu from the Help screen.

2. Click on **A**nnotate... to display a dialog box.

3. Type any notes and reminders of your own. You can even paste text from the clipboard. Then click on **S**ave.

4. A paper clip symbol indicates an annotation for the specific Help topic. Click on it at any time to display your own special notes.

Note
*If you find that you are referring to certain Help topics frequently, select Book**m**ark from the menu and then choose **D**efine to type a Bookmark name. This name will then be associated with the displayed Help topic. The next time you want to access the same help-screen, click on the Book**m**ark menu and then on your Bookmark name to display the topic immediately.*

CHAPTER 6

General and Network Accessories

THIS CHAPTER COVERS

- Opening the Accessories Group
- Using Write
- Using Paintbrush
- Using Notepad
- Using Clock
- Using Cardfile
- Using Calendar
- Using Calculator
- Using Terminal
- Using Recorder
- Using Character Map
- Using Media Player
- Using Sound Recorder
- Opening the Network Group
- Using Chat
- Using NetWatcher
- Using WinMeter
- Using WinPopup
- Logging Off
- Logging On
- Remote Access
- Network Setup
- Fax Facilities

in easy steps

Chapter 6. General and Network Accessories

Opening the Accessories Group

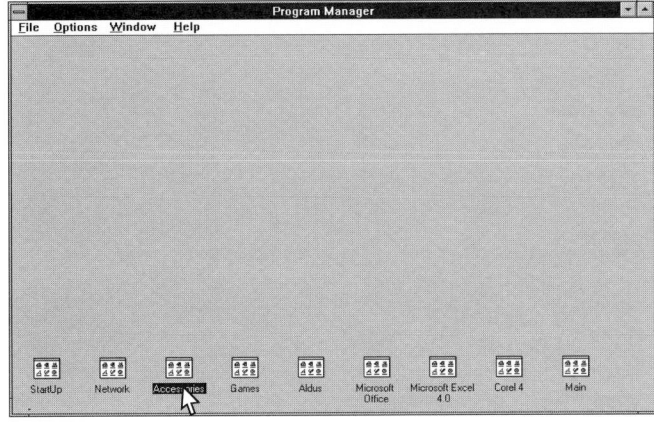

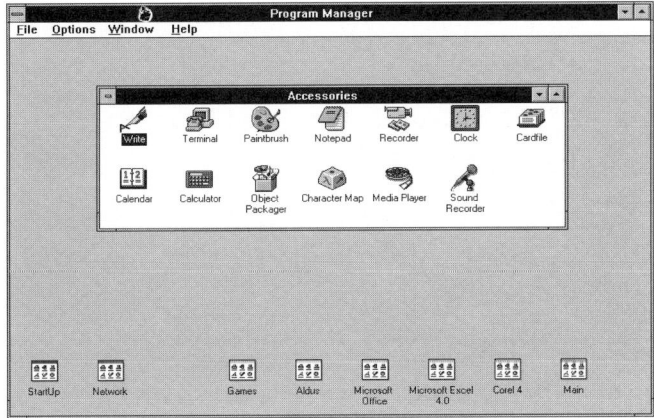

1. Double-click on the Accessories group window.

Note
Enlarge and move the Accessories window to see all the desktop programs icons you can use. Alternatively, use the scroll-bars, which only appear if all the icons are not completely visible. The next few pages describe each accessory in turn.

Using Write

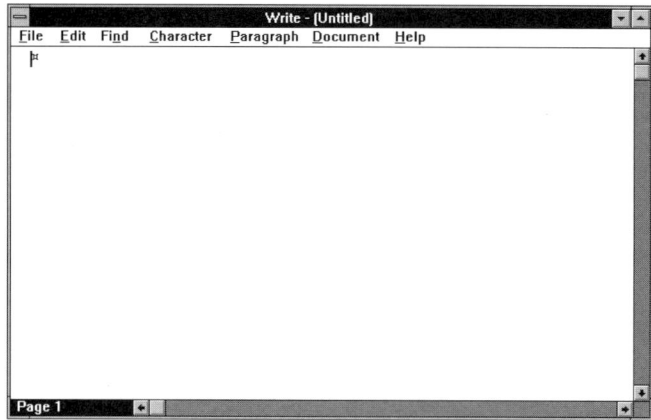

Note

Write is a basic word processor used to create and edit documents.

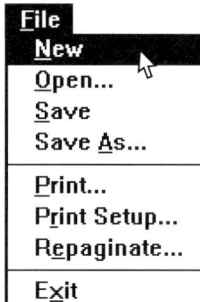

1. Double-click on the Write icon to display the Write application window.

2. Click on the **F**ile menu and then on **O**pen... to open a document for editing. Write documents usually have an extension of WRI.

3. To create a new document, simply start typing. The **N**ew option from the menu will clear the current document area and allow you to create another new document.

4. Use Save **A**s... to save your document for the first time by giving it a name. Then just use **S**ave to save any changes that may be made.

1. To edit text, place the I-beam (cursor) at the start of the text by moving the mouse. Then click on the mouse and drag it to the end of the text-string you want to edit. The selected piece of text will be highlighted.

2. Press the Del key to delete the selected text or type in some new text to replace it.

3. To move the selected text to another part of your document or to another document, click on the **E**dit

menu and choose Cu**t**. Then position the mouse in another area by clicking there and select **P**aste from the **E**dit menu.

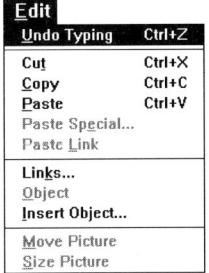

4. To make another copy of the text rather than moving it, follow the procedure in 3 above, except choose **C**opy rather than Cu**t**.

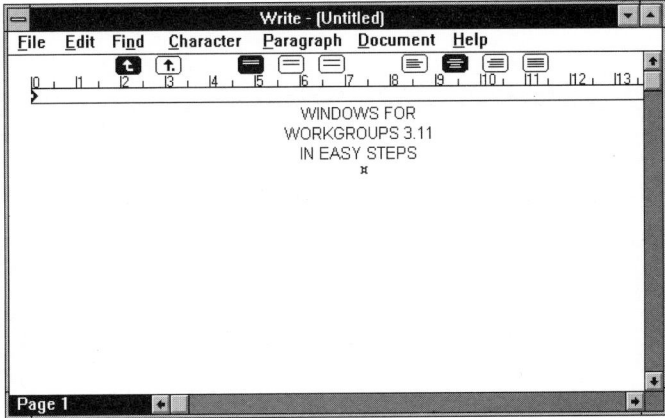

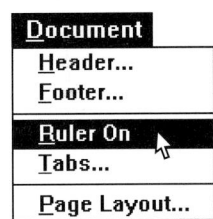

1. Click on the **D**ocument menu and then on **R**uler On to display a ruler at the top. Also at the top are a group of icons used to control tabs, spacing and text alignment.

Note
Instead of using icons on the ruler, click on the Paragraph menu to perform the same functions

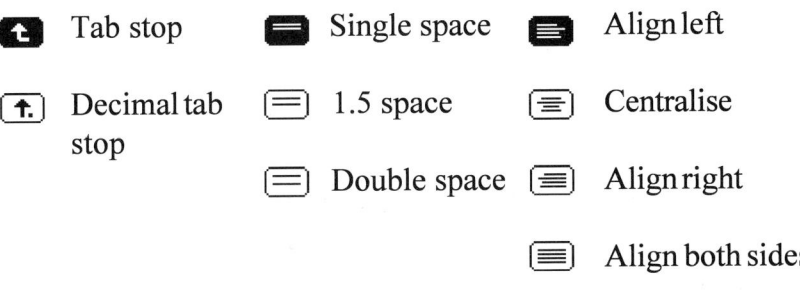

- Tab stop
- Decimal tab stop
- Single space
- 1.5 space
- Double space
- Align left
- Centralise
- Align right
- Align both sides

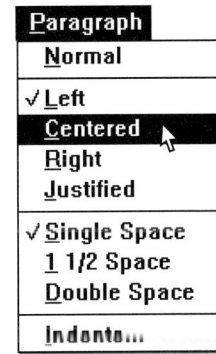

2. As an example, as shown above, drag the mouse over some text to highlight it and then click on the Centralise icon.

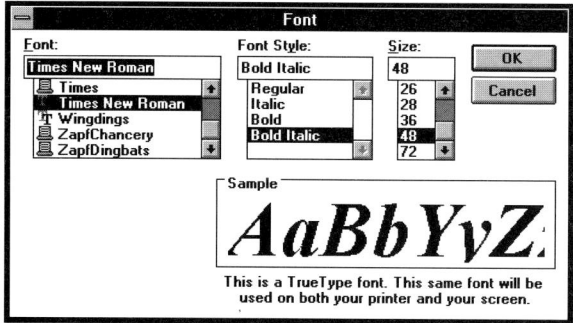

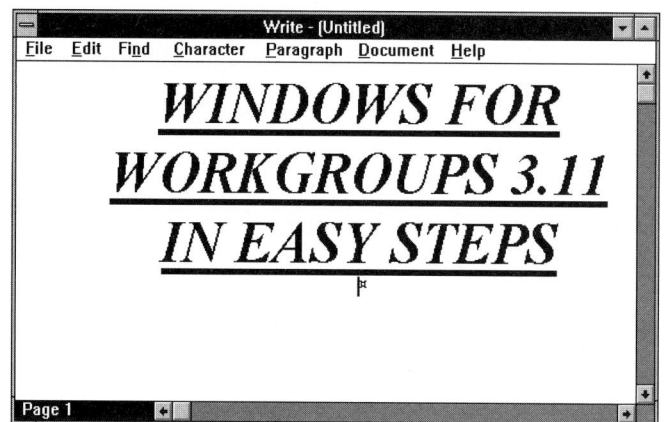

Note

In the Font box you will find some font names prefixed by TT. These are new types of fonts called TrueType. They can be scaled to any size and print exactly as you see them on your screen.

Note

Remember that to change the typeface of existing text, select it first by dragging the mouse over it and highlighting it.

1. To change or use a new typeface for the text, click on the Fonts... option from the Character menu.

2. Select a Font, its style and point size by clicking on the appropriate choices. A sample of what the text will look like is displayed. Click on OK.

3. Use other options in the Character menu to further change the text if required. e.g. Underline. You can even click on Enlarge Font or Reduce Font to change the point size of a font to the next size up or down. If the text is selected, then you'll be able to see the effect of changing point sizes immediately.

Using Paintbrush

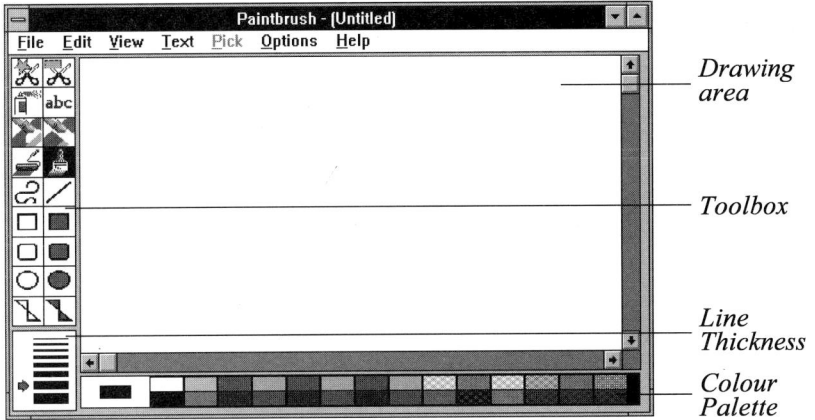

Paintbrush

Note
Paintbrush is a basic drawing and painting graphics program. It can also be used to enhance images scanned using a scanner.

1. Double-click on the Paintbrush icon to display the Paintbrush application window.

2. Click on the required square from the Toolbox to perform a specific function as shown below.

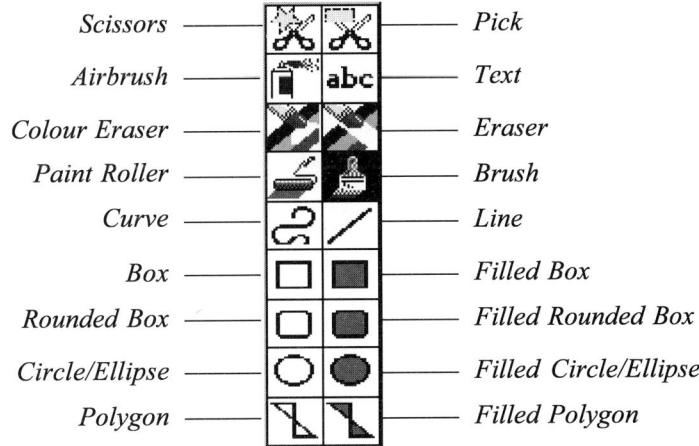

3. Also click inside the Line thickness box to select the appropriate thickness of line to draw/erase with.

4. Click on a box from the colour palette to select the main colour. Click with the right mouse button to select the background colour.

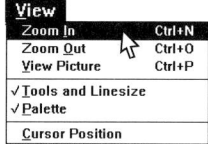

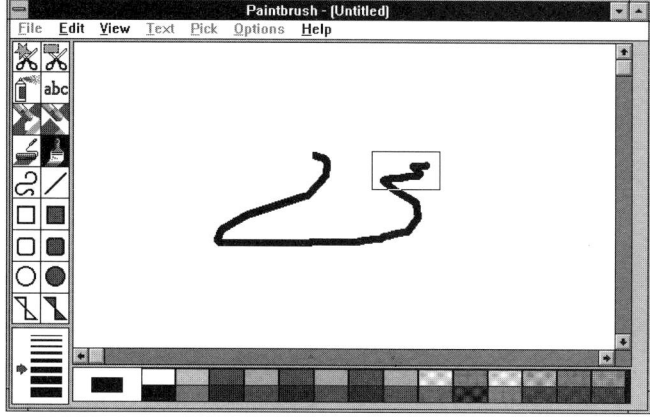

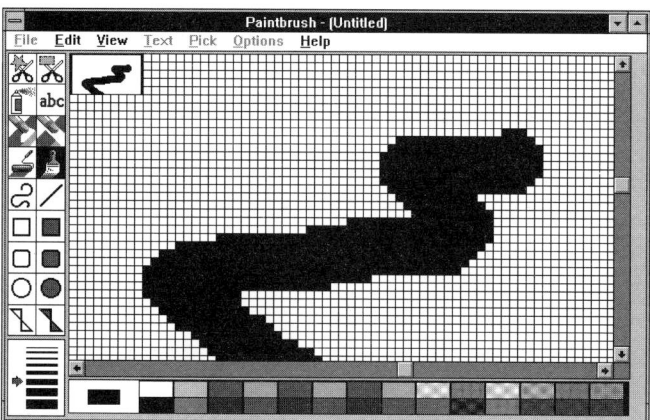

Note

Select Zoom Out from the View menu to get back to the normal display.

1. After drawing a shape, click on the View menu.

2. Click on the Zoom In option. A rectangular box will then appear on the screen.

3. Move your mouse to position the box on the part of the picture you want to zoom into and click.

4. Edit the image by clicking on the grid boxes. Click with the left button to change a box into the foreground colour and with the right button to change it to background colour.

Using Notepad

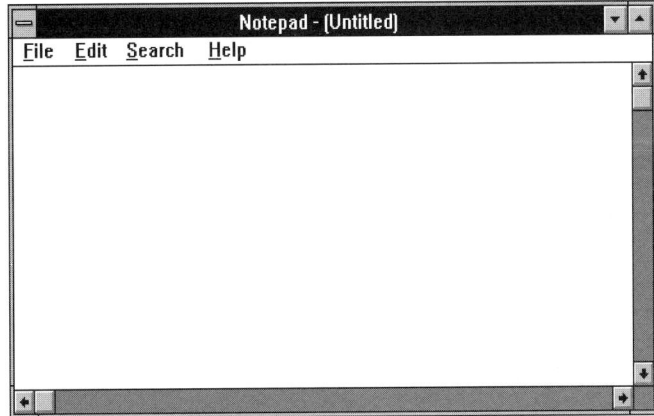

Notepad

Note
Notepad is a simple text editor used to create notes, memos and other basic text files.

1. Double-click on the Notepad icon to display the Notepad Application window.

2. Click on the **E**dit menu to perform cut and paste activities as well as to insert the current date/time. Also, enable **W**ord Wrap to automatically move words to the next line when they reach the right edge of the Notepad window.

3. Click on the **S**earch menu to find the first and subsequent occurrences of a word or phrase in your notepad document.

Tip
The Notepad will not allow you to create very large documents - no more than 50,000 characters (approximately).

Using Clock

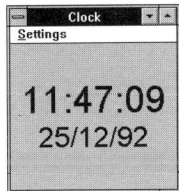 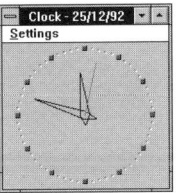

1. Double-click on the Clock icon

2. From the **S**ettings menu click on **A**nalog or **D**igital to change the clock display accordingly.

Tip
By default the clock stays on top when you start other applications so that you can check the time as you work. It works even when the clock window is minimised.

Using Cardfile

Cardfile

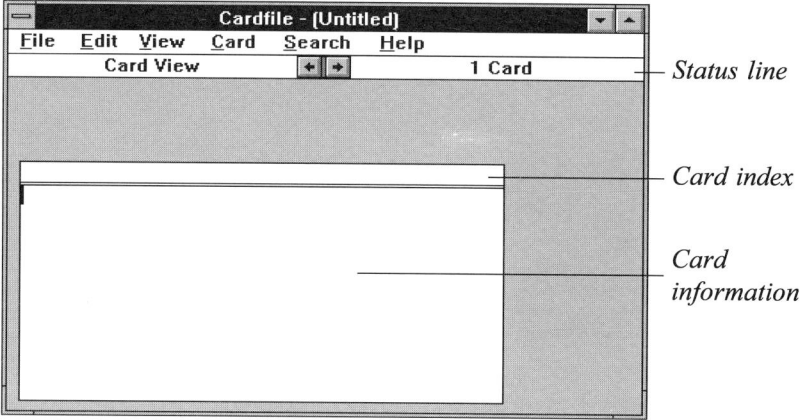

Status line
Card index
Card information

Note
Cardfile lets you store the type of information kept on a manual card index. Examples include Names, Addresses and Phone numbers.

1. Double-click on the Cardfile icon to display the Cardfile window as shown above.

2. To create new cards, click on **N**ew from the **F**ile menu and type the details in the Card information area. e.g. Address.

3. Double-click on the Card index line to display an index dialog box. Type in the index for the card. e.g. Name.

4. To create more cards, click on **A**dd from the **C**ard menu. The Add dialog box is displayed. Type the Card index here and click on OK. Then the card is displayed and you can type the main details in the Card information area.

Shortcut
PgUp and PgDn.

5. Click on the Forward or the Backward arrow in the Status line to look through information in a set of cards.

Tip
Click on List from the View menu to display just the index of all cards alphabetically.

6. Click on the **S**earch menu to look for a specific card. The **G**o To... option will allow you to type in a card index. If a card with the same index exists it will be displayed. Alternatively, the **F**ind... option will allow you to find a match for a word or a phrase from text in the card information area.

7. Use the **F**ile menu to print and save your cardfile.

Using Calendar

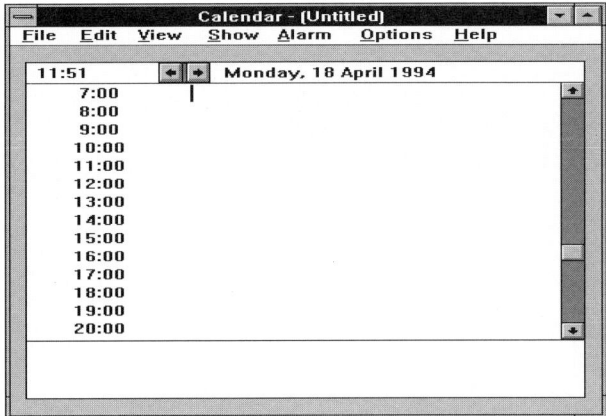

Calendar

Tip
Calendar provides a basic daily/monthly planner. Use Schedule+ which has more features (see Chapter 7).

1. Double-click on the Calendar icon to display today's day planner. Type any text required next to the time.

2. Click on the left or the right arrows near the top to look at other days.

3. Click on **D**ay Settings... from the **O**ptions menu to change the time intervals. You can also insert your own time by selecting **S**pecial Time... from the **O**ptions menu.

4. To set an alarm, first click on the relevant time. Then select the **A**larm menu and click on Set. A small 'bell' symbol will prefix the time that the alarm is set for.

5. Click on **M**onth from the **V**iew menu to display a monthly planner. Double-click on a day from it to display a daily planner for that day.

6. Click on the left or the right arrows near the top to look at other months.

Tip
You can have as many calendars as you want - just save them under different names. For example, have one for Business and another one for personal use!

Note
*The **C**ontrols... option (also from the **A**larm menu) will allow you to ring the alarm up to 10 minutes before the time.*

Today's Date

Selected Date

Using Calculator

Calculator

Note
The Calculator provides both Standard and Scientific calculators.

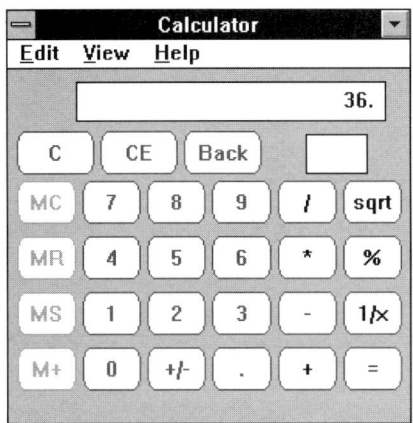

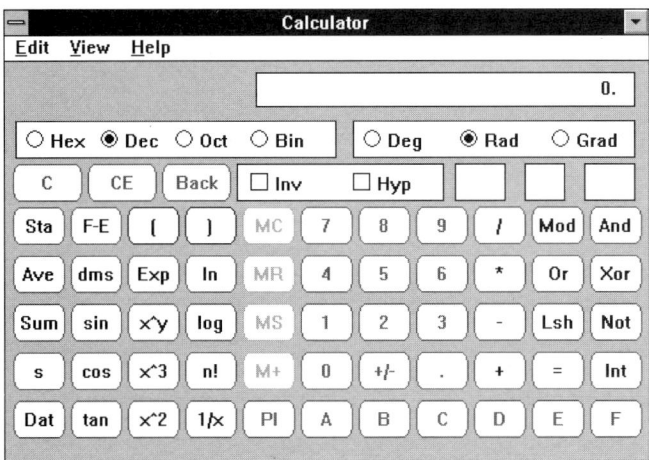

1. Double-click on the Calculator icon to display the standard calculator.

2. Click on the relevant buttons (similar to buttons on a hand-held calculator) or type the values from your keyboard.

3. Click on **S**cientific from the **V**iew menu to display the scientific calculator. Here you will be able to perform trigonometric and statistical operations too.

Using Terminal

Terminal allows your personal computer to communicate with another and transfer information via telephone lines. You will require a modem (MOdulator-DEModulator) to be able to use this facility.

Terminal

A modem is a device that translates computer signals into telephone ones and vice versa. Use Terminal to set up the protocols, or rules, governing the transmission.

Using Recorder

If you seem to be performing the same windows operations frequently, than you need to use the Recorder. It allows you to save a sequence of keystrokes and mouse operations as a macro file. Then when you need to next perform the same operations, just run the appropriate macro and the saved sequence will be executed automatically.

Recorder

Using Character Map

The Character Map enables you to use characters and special symbols from other character sets in your document.

Character Map

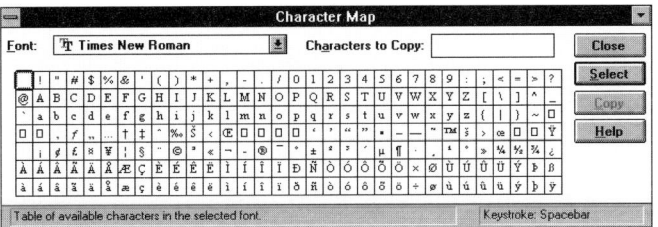

Click on the character required and then click on the **S**elect button. Select as many characters required and then click on the **C**opy button to transfer them to the Windows clipboard.

Note
A Clipboard is a temporary storage area. Choose Paste from the Edit menu to copy its contents in your application.

Using Media Player

Media Player

This is a multimedia accessory program. Multimedia is the integration of text, graphics, video and sound. Provided you have the necessary sound card and speakers, and the sound drivers installed, you can use Media Player to play sound/animation files and multimedia devices.

Using Sound Recorder

Sound Recorder

Sound Recorder is another multimedia accessory program. Like the Media Player you will need the necessary hardware and software installed before you can make use of it, including a microphone attached to your sound card.

Sound Recorder will allow you to record, edit and play sound files. It has buttons similar to a tape recorder, except here you will click on them using a mouse. These buttons are Rewind, Fast Forward, Play, Stop and Record.

Chapter 6. General and Network Accessories

Opening the Network Group

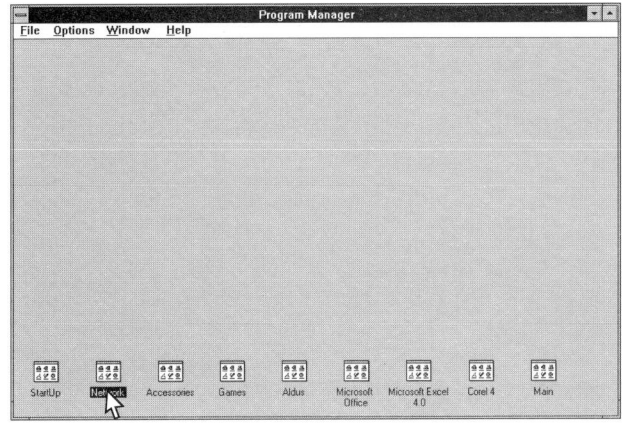

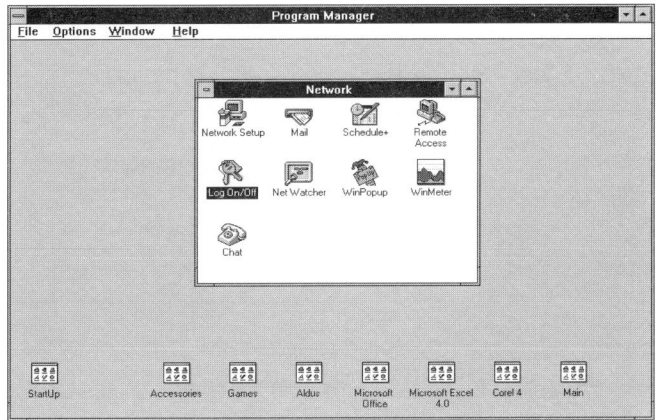

1. Double-click on the Network group icon.

Note
Enlarge and move the Network window to see all the program icons you can use. Alternatively, use the scrollbars, which only appear if all the icons are not completely visible. The next few pages describe each Newwork accessory in turn.

Note
Mail and Schedule+ are described in Chapter 7.

Using Chat

Note

Chat allows you to hold conversations with people as though you were on the phone to them. What you type appears on their screen and vice versa.

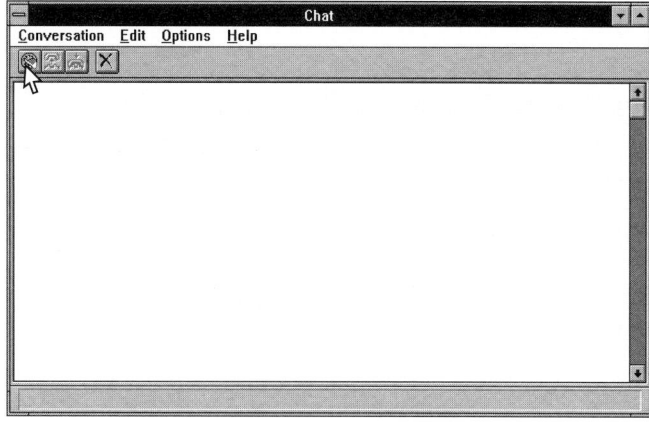

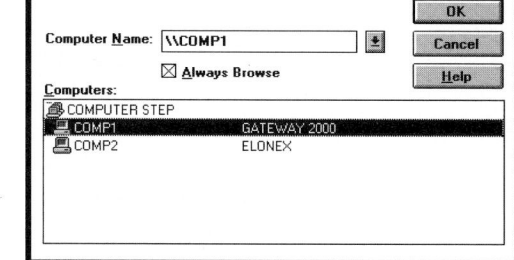

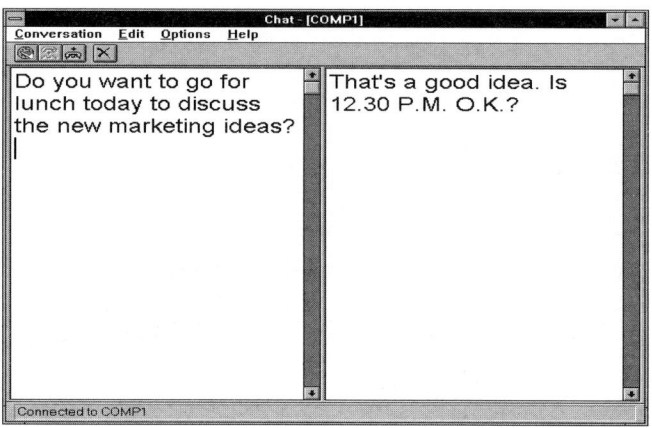

Chapter 6. General and Network Accessories   **143**

1. Double-click on the Chat icon in the Network group. The Chat screen then appears.

2. To send a message, click on the Dial button on the Toolbar or select **D**ial... from the **C**onversation menu. The Select Computer dialog box then appears.

3. Click on the computer name you want to send a message to. Clicking on a Workgroup icon will show all members of that workgroup. Then click on OK.

4. The status bar at the bottom of the screen will tell you whether the other user is answering. When the call is answered, the screen will split into two sections. One is for your text, the other is for the other person's reply.

Note
*To answer a call, simply click on the Answer button or select **A**nswer from the **C**onversation menu.*

5. If you wish to add another person to a Chat conversation, simply click on the Dial button and select the approptiate computer name. When the person answers, the screen will be further split to allow them to write messages.

6. To finish a Chat conversation, click on the Hang-up button or select **H**ang-up from the **C**onversation menu.

Note
You can have up to seven others involved in the conversation, but only the original sender of the message can add the extra people.

1. Select the **O**ptions menu to customise Chat.

2. Choose **F**ont... or Background **C**olor... to display dialog boxes which let you choose how Chat appears.

3. Choose **P**references... to display the Preferences dialog box which lets you decide on the screen layout. Click on '**A**utostart Chat when called' if you want the Chat screen to appear each time you receive a call.

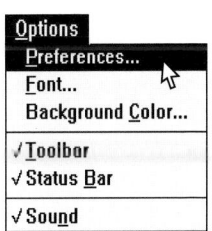

Using NetWatcher

Full access

Read-only access

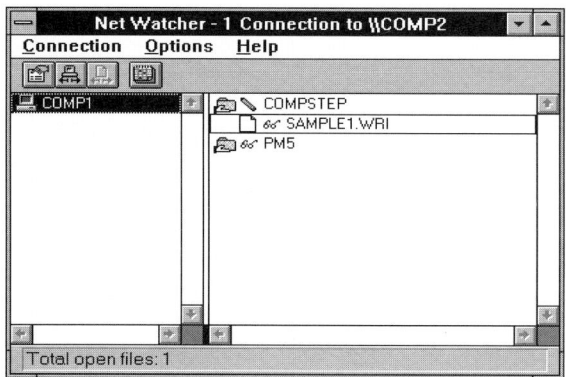

1. Double-click on the NetWatcher icon in the Network group. The NetWatcher screen then appears and displays a list of everyone using your facilities and what they are using. A pencil icon is used to show where someone has full access and a pair of glasses shows read-only access.

Using WinMeter

Tip
To alter the performance priority between your applications and the shared resources of your computer, select the Startup button, after first selecting the Network icon in the Control Panel group from the Main program group.

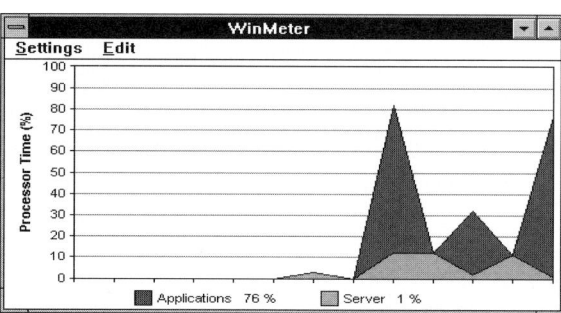

1. Click on the WinMeter icon in the Network group. This displays a screen showing the allocation of your computer's memory to your own activities and also of others sharing your facilities.

Using WinPopup

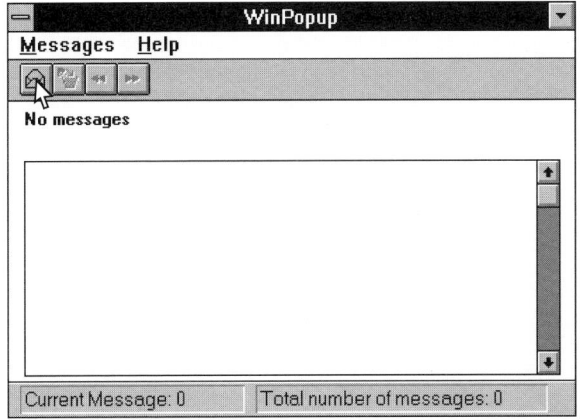

Note

WinPopup allows you to send simple messages to other users on your network. Your computer can also use it to inform you of events such as a document finishing printing.

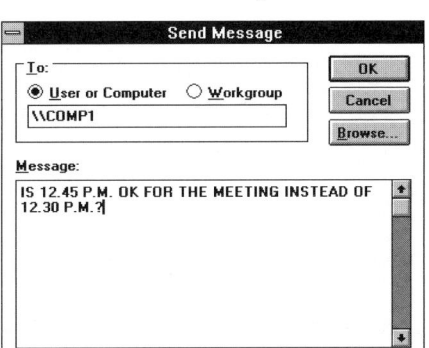

Note

*Select the **B**rowse... button to select the computer you want to send the message to.*

1. Click on the WinPopup icon in the Network group. The WinPopup screen then appears.

2. Click on the Send button on the Toolbar (or select **S**end... from the **M**essages menu). The Send Message dialog box then appears. Select '**U**ser or Computer' or '**W**orkgroup' option to send a message to all workgroup members.

3. Type your message in the message box and then click on OK. Your message will then be sent to the computer specified or all members of the workgroup.

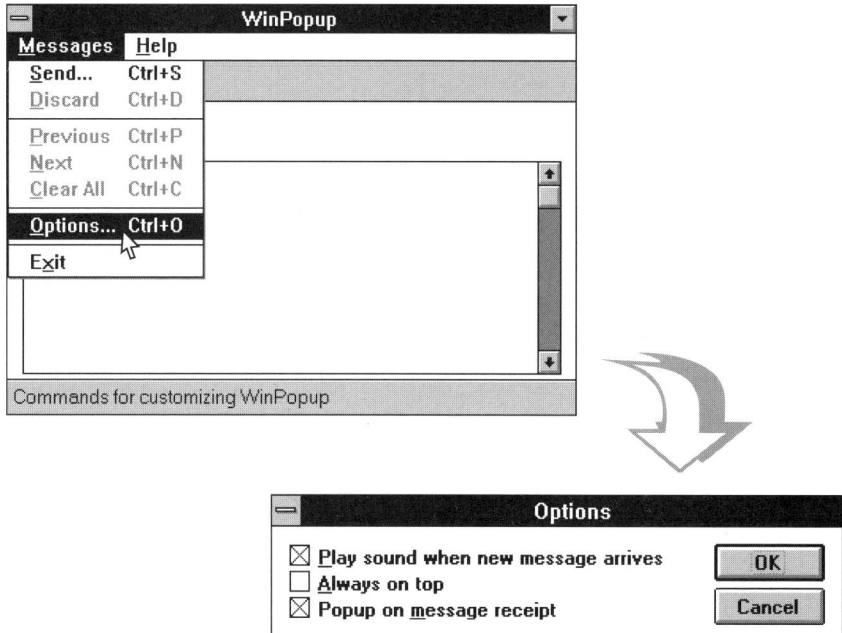

1. Select **O**ptions... from the **M**essages menu. The Options dialog box will be displayed.

2. Select the '**P**lay sound when new message arrives' check box to have the computer make a bleep when you are sent a message.

3. Select the '**A**lways on top' check box if you want the program to popup on top of whatever you are working on when a message is received.

4. Select the 'Popup on **m**essage receipt' box to have the WinPopup screen maximise when you recieve a message.

Tip

*You must have WinPopup running to be able to receive messages. To start up WinPopup each time you Log on, select the Network icon from the Control Panel in the Main group. Click on the **S**tartup button and check the Enable **W**inPopup on Startup box.*

Logging Off

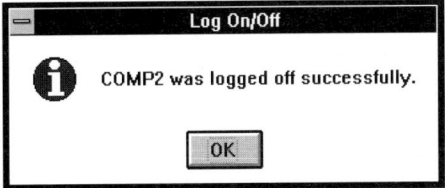

1. Double-click on the Logon/off icon in the Network group. A box will appear to tell you that you have been logged off. You will still be able to use your computer and others will still be able to use your computer's shared facilities, but you will not be able to use shared facilities on other computers.

Tip
You can use the Logon/off facility to allow more than one person access to the same computer. They just need to have different Logon names and Passwords.

Logging On

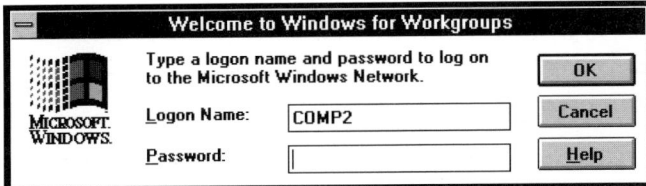

1. Double click on the Logon/off icon in the Network group. The Welcome to Windows for Workgroups dialog box then appears.

2. Enter your **P**assword and click on OK and you will be logged back on to your computer and able to use shared facilities again.

Remote Access

This lets you log on to your computer from another location such as your home. To do this you need to have a special network server or remote access server connected to your WFWG network.

Remote Access

Network Setup

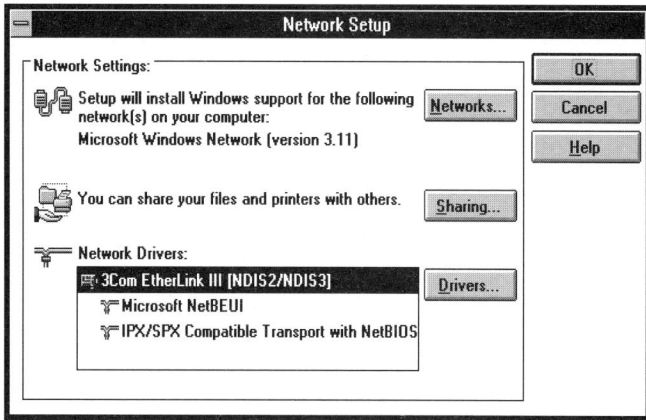

1. Double-click on the Network Setup icon in the Network group. The Network Setup screen will appear, which allows you to modify the setting of your network.

2. To install new networks, click on the **N**etworks... button.

3. To stop or start sharing your files and printers, click on the **S**haring... button and check the appropriate boxes.

4. To Install or modify the network driver software which controls the network card in your computer click on the **D**rivers... button.

Fax Facilities

Windows for Workgroups includes the Microsoft At Work PC Fax software, which lets you send and receive faxes via fax machines and computers equiped with fax modems. To use this facility you must have a fax modem connected to your computer or have access to a shared fax modem. The Fax icon in the Control Panel screen can be used to control the installation and sharing of fax modems. The Mail facility (which is described in Chapter 7) is used to send and read faxes.

CHAPTER 7
Mail and Schedule+

- Setting up a Workgroup Postoffice
- Adding a User to the Postoffice
- Changing User Information
- Removing a User
- Getting into Mail
- Sending a Message
- Message Options
- Reading/Replying to Mail Messages
- Deleting Mail Messages
- Creating New Folders
- Moving Messages between Folders
- Forwarding Messages
- Exiting from Mail
- Getting into Schedule+
- Adding Appointments
- Adding Recurring Appointments
- Using the Task List
- Scheduling a Meeting
- Exiting from Schedule+

Setting up a Workgroup Postoffice

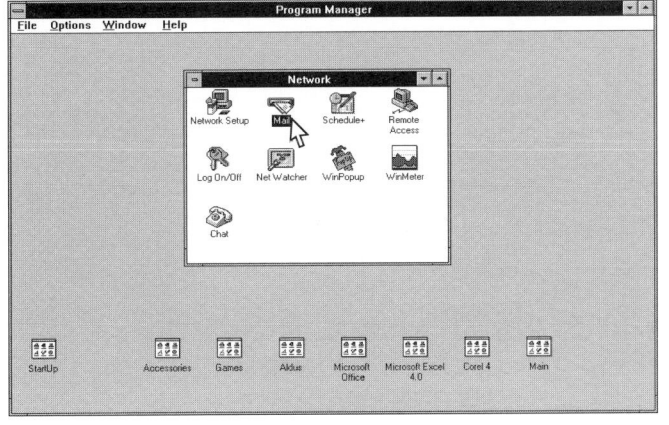

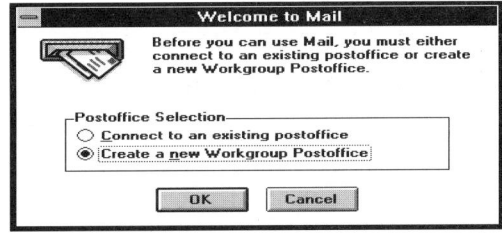

Note

One of the members of a Workgroup (the administrator) must set up a Postoffice before anyone can use the Mail or Schedule+ facilities. A Postoffice takes up 360K of hard disk space plus 16K for each user account on the administrators PC.

Note

You can only have one Postoffice for each workgroup.

1. Double-click on the Mail icon in the Network group. The Welcome to Mail dialog box appears.

2. Click on Create a new Workgroup Postoffice and then click on OK. Click on Yes in the Mail warning box and the Create Workgroup Postoffice dialog box will be displayed.

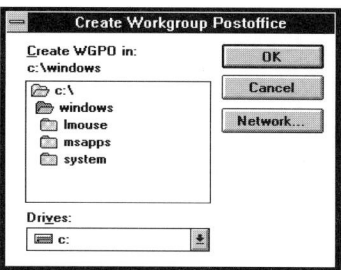

3. Highlight the directory where you want the Postoffice to be located and click on OK. A dialog box appears asking you to fill in your Administrator Account Details.

4. When you have done this click on OK. A warning box will be displayed which tells you where the Postoffice is to be created. Click on OK.

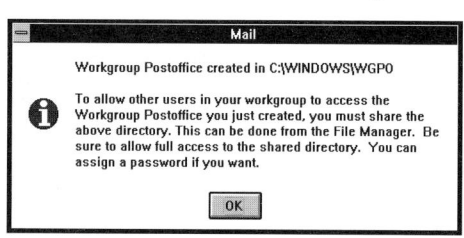

Note

You need to share the workgroup Postoffice directory with everyone who is going to use Mail.

5. Go into File Manager and select the WGPO directory.

6. Click on the Share Directory button. In the Share As dialog box choose *F*ull as the Access type (use a Fu*l*l Access password if desired) and check the Re-share at Start*u*p box.

7. Click on OK and the directory will be shared.

Adding a User to the Postoffice

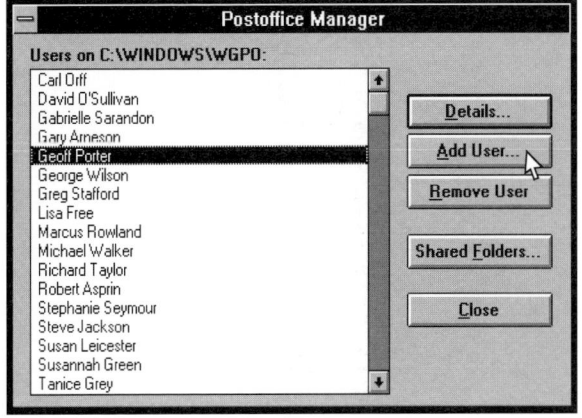

Note
Users have to be added to the Mail system before they can sign in and use the mail facilities.

1. Select **P**ostoffice Manager... from the **M**ail menu. The Postoffice Manager screen will appear, displaying a list of users.

2. Click on the **A**dd User button. The Add User dialog box will be displayed. Complete the user's details and click on OK. The user will then be added to the user list on the Postoffice Manager screen.

Note
*Only the Adminstrator has access to **P**ostoffice Manager.*

Changing User Information

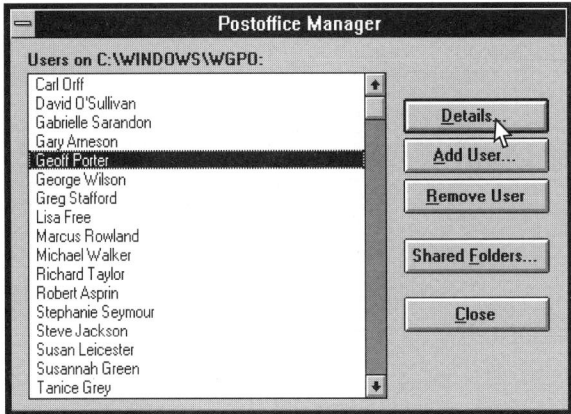

Note

This method can be used to change the password for a user who has forgotten it.

1. In the Postoffice Manager screen, select the user whose details you want to change. Click on **D**etails... and a dialog box will appear showing the user's details.

2. Click on the details you want to change and make your alterations. Click on OK and the user's details will be changed.

Removing a User

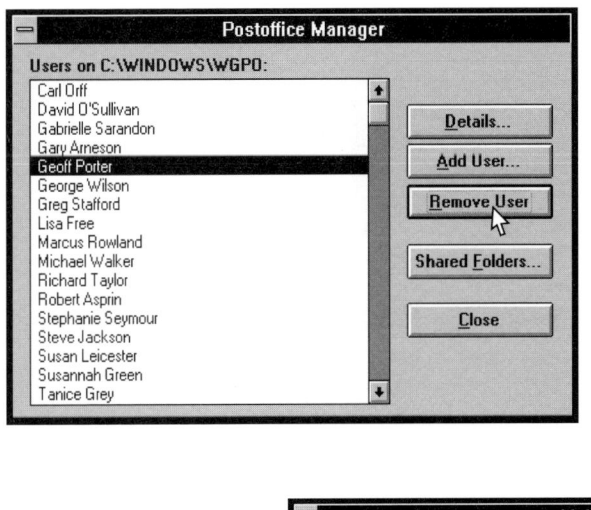

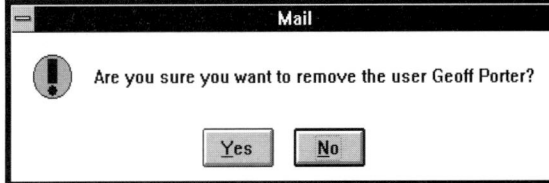

1. In Postoffice Manager, select the user you wish to remove. Click on **R**emove User and a box will appear asking if you are sure.

2. Click on **Y**es and the user will be removed from the user list and will no longer be able to use Mail and Schedule+.

Note
The Postoffice administrator cannot remove their own account this way. To do this you must remove the WGPO directory from your hard disk.

Getting into Mail

Note

The amount of hard disk space taken up by Mail messages may vary from say just 100K to several megabytes.

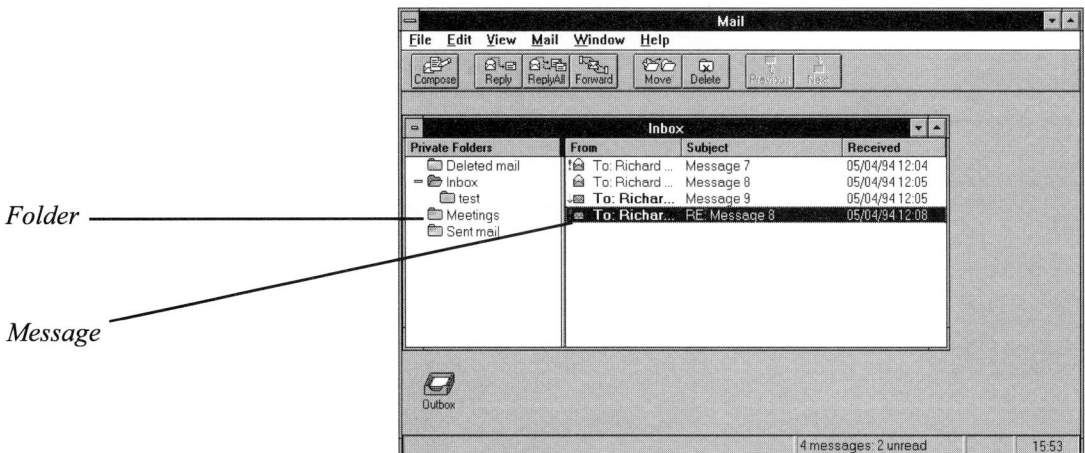

Folder

Message

1. Double-click on the Mail icon in the Network group. The Mail Sign In dialog box then appears.

Note
The first time you sign in to mail the Welcome to Mail dialog box will be displayed. You should select 'Connect to an existing Postoffice' and click on OK. The Mail Sign In dialog box will then appear.

2. Type in your password and click on OK. The Mail screen will be displayed.

Chapter 7. Mail and Schedule+

Sending a Message

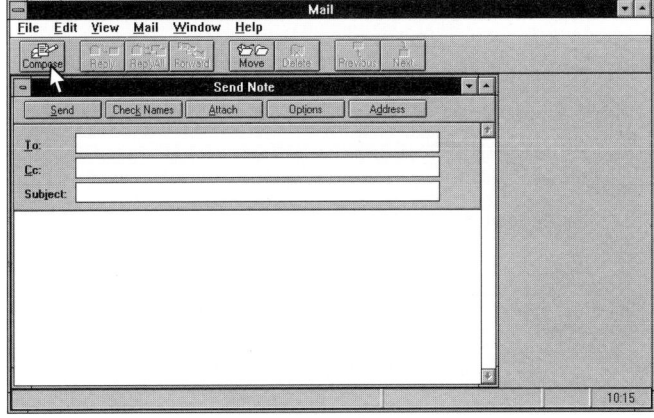

1. Click on the Compose button on the Toolbar or select Compose **N**ote from the **M**ail menu. The Send Note screen appears.

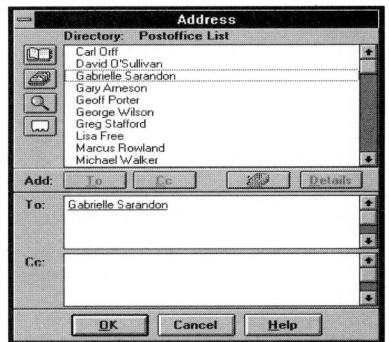

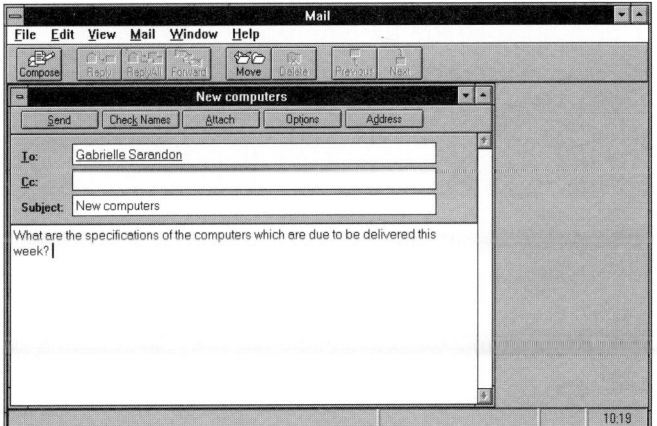

Tip

*If you want to find out about someone you are sending a message to, click on the **D**etails button and information about the user will be displayed.*

2. Click on the A**d**dress button to select the recipients of the message. The Address dialog box appears.

3. Select the name of someone you want to send the message to by double-clicking on their name in the list or by clicking on it and then clicking on **T**o. This will place the name in the 'To:' box at the bottom of the screen.

4. When you have selected all the recipients of the message, then click on OK. You will be returned to the Send Note screen with the names you have selected put into the 'To:' box.

Note
Using the method described in steps 3 and 4 you can include names in the 'Cc:' box if you want to send a courtesy copy of the message.

Tip

*If you need to regularly send the same message to several people, set Personal **G**roups... from the **M**ail menu to include your recipients and then simply select the group name to send messages to them all.*

5. Click in the Sub**j**ect: box and type in a description of the message to help the recipients know what it is about.

6. Click in the text box and type your message.

7. You can send files with your message by clicking on the **A**ttach button. The Attach dialog box is displayed. Use the drive and directory boxes to find a file you wish to send and click on it to select it.

8. When you have selected the file you want, click on **A**ttach. Select more files if required, clicking on **A**ttach each time. Finally click on **C**lose and you will return to the Send Note screen. Icons representing the files you are sending will appear in the message area.

9. Click on the **S**end button and the message will be sent.

Note
*You can send Mail messages from File Manager by selecting **S**end Mail... from the **M**ail menu.*

Message Options

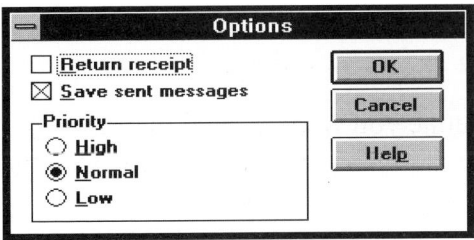

1. In the Send Note screen click on the Options button. The Options dialog box is displayed.

2. Click on the **R**eturn receipt check box if you want a message sent back to you when the recipient reads the message.

3. Click on the **S**ave sent messages check box if you want a copy of each message you send saved in the Sent Mail folder.

4. You can specify a priority for the message to indicate to the recipient how important the message is. The default is **N**ormal, but you can select **H**igh or **L**ow priority. When a message with High or Low priority appears in a recipients' message folder it has a special icon.

   High Priority

   Low Priority

Note
Sent Mail is one of the 3 private folders included in your basic Mail setup.

Reading/Replying to Mail Messages

Note
New Mail messages appear in your In-Box folder. Double-click on the folder to list them.

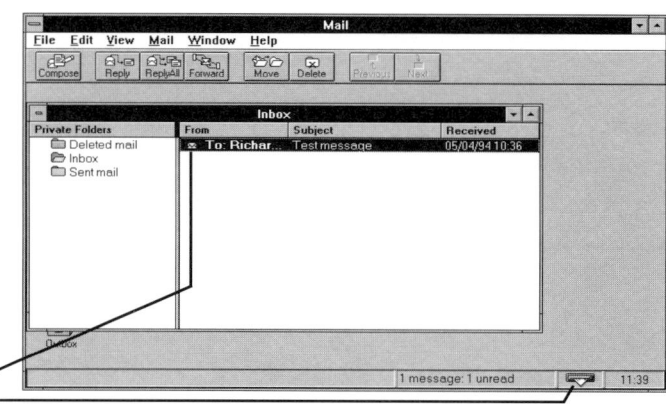

Indicates that you have new mail.

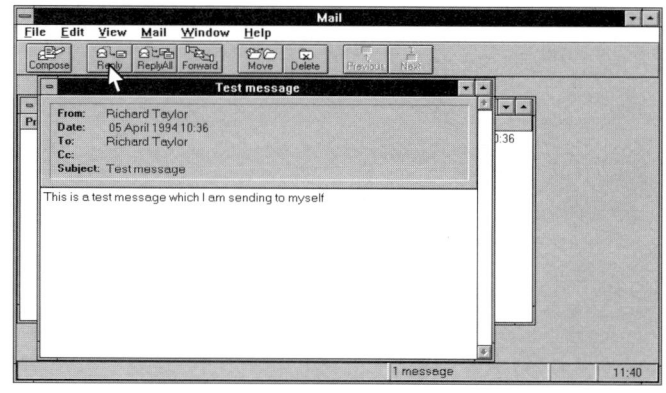

Chapter 7. Mail and Schedule+

1. Double-click on the message you want to read and it will be displayed.

2. If you want to reply to a message, click on the Reply button (or choose **R**eply from the **M**ail menu) which will send your reply to the original sender of the message. A Send Note box then appears displaying information about the original message.

3. Type in your reply and click on the **S**end button to send it.

Tip
Click on the Reply All button (or choose Reply to All from the Mail menu) if you want to send your reply to everyone who received the original message.

Deleting Mail Messages

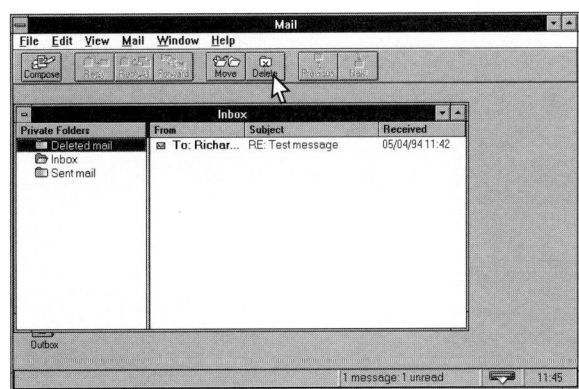

Tip
If you are worried about accidentally erasing important messages you can read them in the Deleted Messages folder before you exit to check that you don't want to keep them.

1. Select the message that you want to delete and click on the Delete button on the Toolbar (or choose **D**elete from the **F**ile menu). The deleted messages will be removed from the current folder and placed in the Deleted Mail folder.

Note
*Messages in the Deleted Mail folder will be erased when you exit Mail unless the '**E**mpty Deleted Mail folder when exiting' check box (found in the Mail Options... dialog box) is cleared.*

Creating New Folders

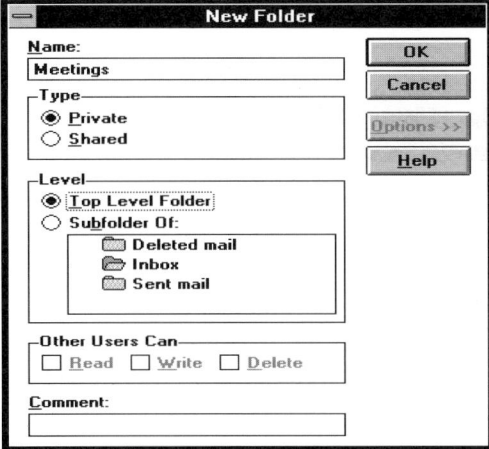

1. Select **N**ew Folder... from the **F**ile menu. The New Folder dialog box is then displayed.

Note

Shared folders are stored in the Workgroup Postoffice and can be used by all members of the workgroup.

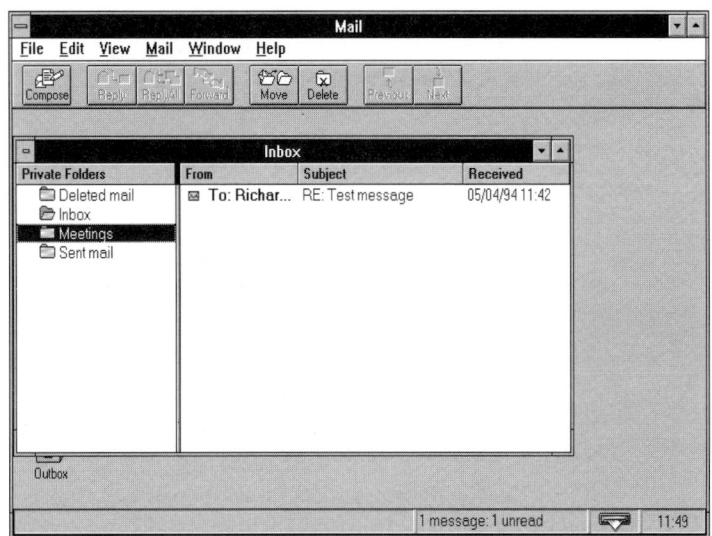

2. Type in a name for the new folder and choose whether it is to be **S**hared by the workgroup or **P**rivate. If you wish to control the access others have to a shared folder or the location in your Mail folder tree, click on **O**ptions and make the appropriate choice. Then click on OK.

Moving Messages between Folders

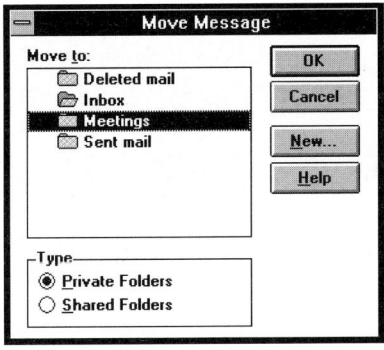

1. Select a message and drag it to the folder you want to move it into. The message will be moved to that folder.

OR

1. Select a message and click on the Move button on the Toolbar or choose **M**ove... from the **F**ile menu. The Move Message dialog box will be displayed. Click on **P**rivate or **S**hared Folders and click on the folder you want to move the message into and click on OK. The message will then be moved to the correct folder.

Note
*Clicking on the **N**ew... button in the Move Message dialog box lets you create a new folder to move the message into.*

Forwarding Messages

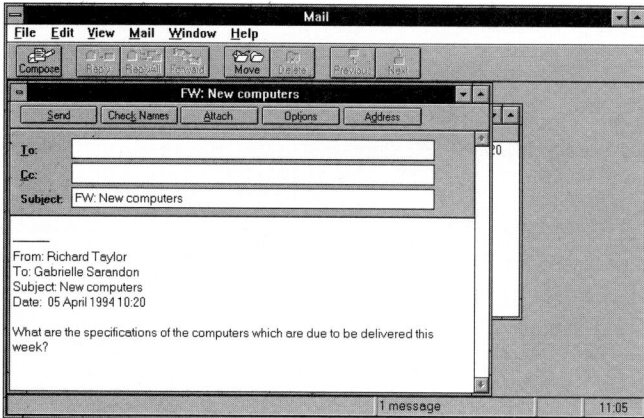

1. Select a message and click on the Forward button or select **F**orward from the **M**ail menu. The message then appears ready to forward.

2. Type the name of the person you are forwarding the message to in the **T**o: box or click on A**d**dress to select names from your address book. Fill in the Sub**j**ect box and click on **S**end. The message will then be forwarded.

Exiting from Mail

1. To exit and sign out from Mail, select Exi**t** and Sign Out from the **F**ile menu. If you choose this option any applications which use Mail, such as Schedule+, will also be closed.

OR

1. To exit and remain signed in, select E**x**it from the **F**ile menu. If you have applications which use Mail, such as Schedule+, running this will allow you to continue using them.

Chapter 7. Mail and Schedule+

Getting into Schedule+

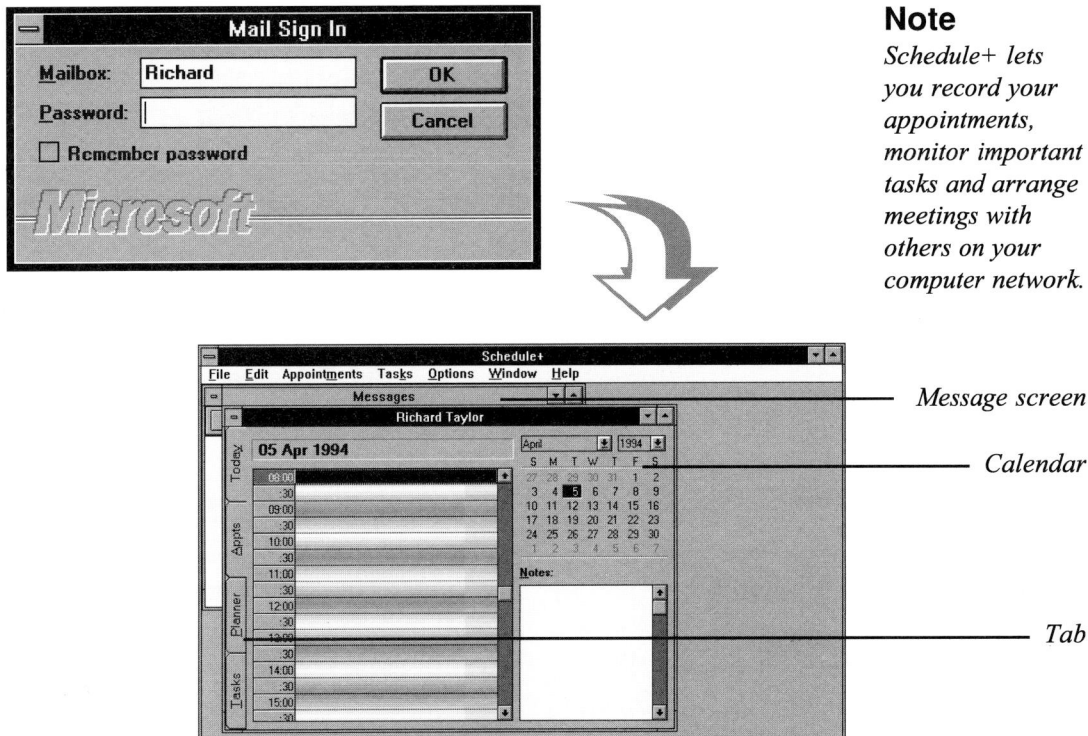

Note
Schedule+ lets you record your appointments, monitor important tasks and arrange meetings with others on your computer network.

1. Double-click on the Schedule+ icon in the Nework group. The Mail Sign In screen then appears.

2. Type in your Mail password and click on OK. The Schedule+ screen then appears showing your appointments for today. Also any meeting reminders you have set for the period since you last logged on will appear.

Adding Appointments

Note
When you add an appointment, that time is blocked out on your planner and so other people can see when you are available for meetings.

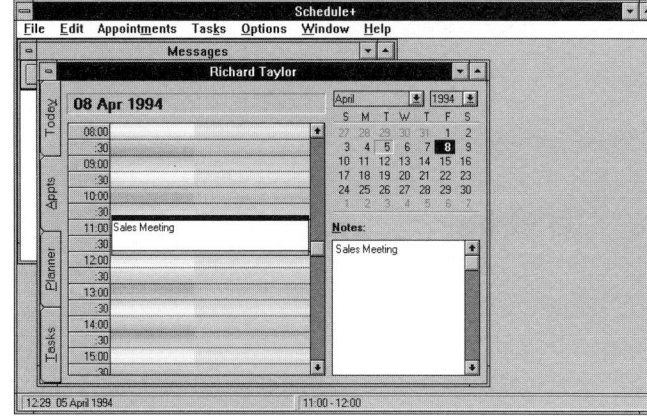

1. Click in the Appointment Book on the time you want the appointment to be set. Drag down to cover the period you want.

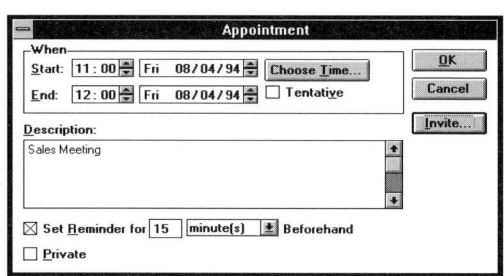

2. Click on **N**ew Appointment... in the Appoint**m**ents menu. The Appointment dialog box then appears.

Note
A tentative appointment is recorded with a grey background and does not appear in your planner when other people look at it.

3. Click on the Tentati**v**e check box if the appointment is not definite.

4. Type a description of the meeting in the **D**escription box.

5. To be warned about the meeting, click on the Set **R**eminder check box and select the warning time. Click on the **P**rivate check box if you want others to know that you are busy but don't want them to see the details of your appointment.

6. If the appointment just involves you, click on OK and it will be recorded in the Appointment Book.

Chapter 7. Mail and Schedule+

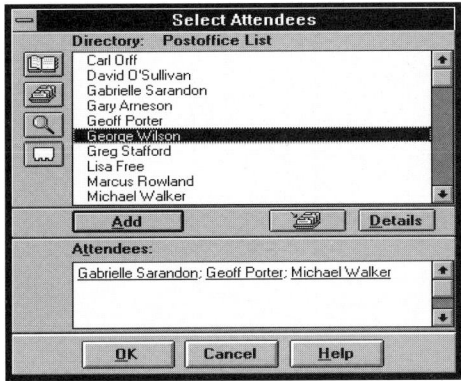

7. If the appointment is a meeting with other people on your computer network, click on **I**nvite... and the Select Attendees dialog box will be displayed.

8. Select the names of the people you wish to attend the meeting, clicking on the **A**dd button after selecting each name. When you have selected all the attendees, click on **O**K and you will return to the Appointment screen.

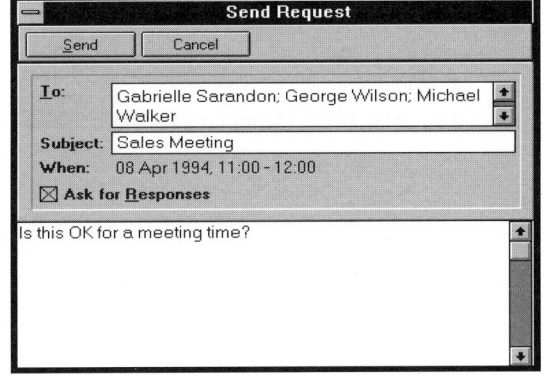

9. Click on OK and the Send Request dialog box is displayed.

10. Type in a subject for the message and then click in the message box and type in a message.

11. Click on the **S**end button and messages will be sent to all the attendees at the meeting.

Note
To modify an existing appointment, click on it and select Edit Appt... from the Edit menu or simply double-click on the appointment.

Appointment Book symbols

Meeting symbol

Private symbol

Reminder symbol

Adding Recurring Appointments

Note

*You can change an existing appointment into a recurring one by selecting it and choosing New **R**ecurring Appt... from the Appoint**m**ents menu.*

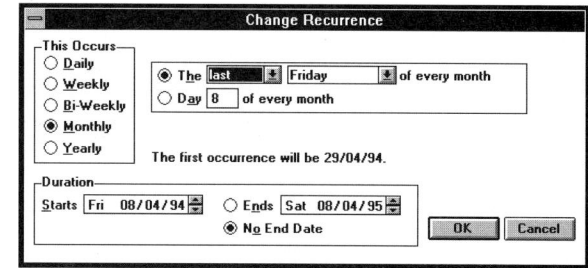

1. In your Appointment Book, click on the time slot for the recurring appointment. Then select New **R**ecurring Appt... from the Appoint**m**ents menu. The Recurring Appointment dialog box will be displayed.

2. Click on the **C**hange... button. The Change Recurrence dialog box is displayed.

3. Click on the appropriate option in the 'This Occurs' column to choose how often the appointment occurs.

Note

The layout here varies depending on the 'This Occurs' option.

4. Click on the box to show which day of the week or date the appointment occurs on.

5. Click on the N**o** End Date option if you want the appointment to recur indefinitely or on the E**n**ds option and use the arrow buttons to select the start and finish dates.

Recurring appointment symbol

6. Click on OK to return to the Recurring Appointment dialog box. Click on OK again and the recurring appointment will be recorded in your Appointment Book.

Using the Task List

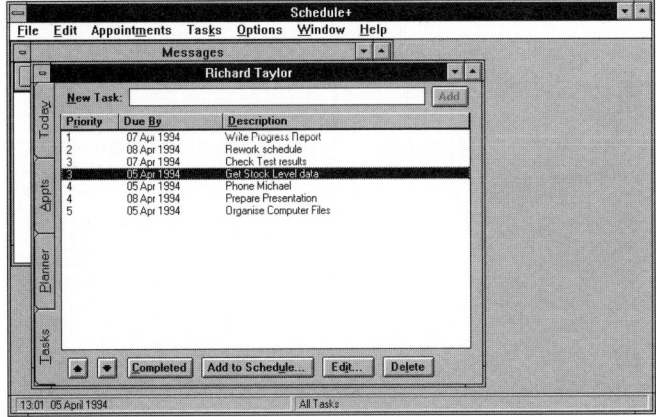

Note
The Task List shows tasks in order of decreasing priority. Overdue tasks are marked in red.

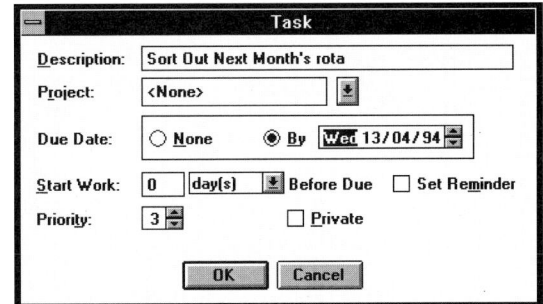

1. Click on the **T**asks tab. The Task List will then appear.

2. To add a task to the list, type a description of it in the **N**ew Task box. Then click on the Add button or press Enter.

3. To add detail to a task, select it by clicking on its description in the Task List and click on the Ed**i**t... button. Or select **E**dit Task... from the **E**dit menu. The Task dialog box is then displayed.

   Shortcut
   Double-click on the task.

4. To change the description of the task, click on the **D**escription box and type your alteration.

5. To associate the task with a particular project, click in the P**r**oject box and type the project name.

6. To select a due date, click on the **B**y option in the Due Date box and select a date by clicking on the arrows.

Note

*To delete a task select it and click on the De*l*ete button. To remove a completed task click on* **C**_ompleted. The completed tasks are recorded in the Notes box of the Appointment Book._

7. To set a reminder to yourself to start a task, click on the **S**tart Work line and type in a number of days/weeks/months and click on the Set Re**m**inder check box.

8. The numbers (1-9) in the Priori**t**y box indicate how important the task is; the lower the number the more important. To change the priority for the task, click on the up arrow to increase the priority or on the down arrow to decrease it.

9. Click on OK and the task will appear in the Task List with any modifications you have made.

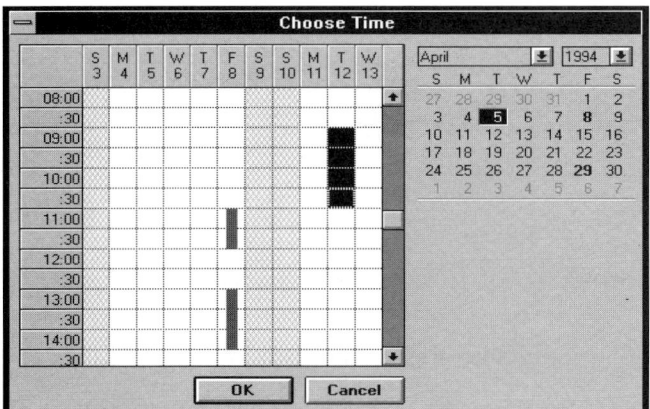

1. To book time in your appointment book for a task, select the task by clicking on it in the Task list and then click on the 'Add to Sched**u**le...' button. The Choose Time dialog box then appears.

2. Select the date for the task using the calendar, click on the time slot and drag down to cover the period you want, then click on OK. The task will then be in your Task List and booked in your Appointment Book.

Scheduling a Meeting

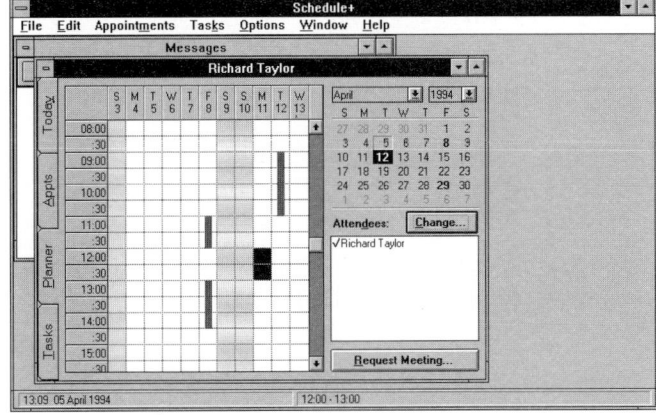

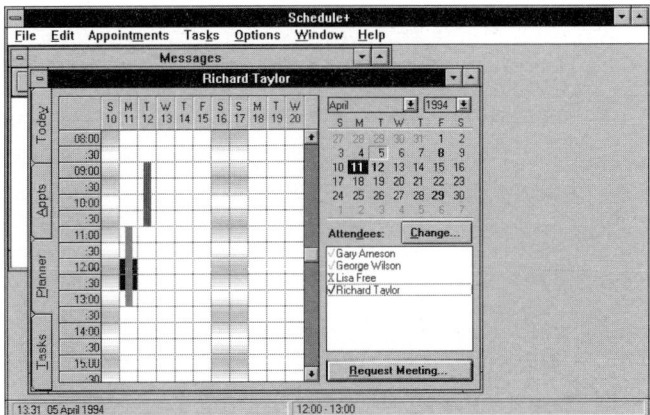

1. You can use Schedule+ to see whether the other attendees are available for a meeting. Click on the **P**lanner Tab. Your Planner will be displayed. The time when you have appointments booked will be blocked out.

2. Click on the **C**hange... button. The Select Attendees dialog box will be displayed. Click on the names of the people you want to attend the meeting and click on **A**dd. When you have selected all the attendees, click on OK.

Note

Only one colour is used to represent the busy times for all the attendees.

3. Your planner will be displayed with your schedule overlaid with that of the other attendees. Busy time slots for the others are shown in a different colour. There is a list of the attendees you have selected in the Atten**d**ees box.

4. Select a time slot for the meeting by clicking on the planner and dragging to increase the length of the meeting if necessary. Then click on the **R**equest Meeting Button. The Send Request dialog box will be displayed.

Note

If any of the attendees are busy at the time you have selected, there will be a cross by their name.

5. Type in a description of the message in the Sub**j**ect box and then click in the message box and type in a message. Then click on the **S**end button and messages will be sent to all the attendees at the meeting. When Schedule+ has successfully sent all the messages, the meeting will be shown in your Appointment Book.

Exiting from Schedule+

1. To exit from Schedule+ and sign out from Mail, select 'Exi**t** and Sign Out' from the **F**ile menu.

OR

1. To exit from Schedule+ and keep running Mail, select E**x**it from the **F**ile menu.

Note

*If you choose to 'Exi**t** and Sign Out', any reminders for appointments which occur before you next use Schedule+ will not be displayed.*

# CHAPTER 8

Object Linking and Embedding

THIS CHAPTER COVERS

- What is OLE?
- Linking an Object
- Embedding an Object
- Changing a Linked Object
- Changing an Embedded Object
- Using Object Packager

What is OLE?

Object Linking and Embedding, or OLE for short, allows your applications to share information (referred to as objects). An object can be a piece of text, drawing, spreadsheet cell, sound file, or any other type of information. Before using OLE, you will need to check if your applications support it. Examples of applications that do, include Windows Write and Paintbrush, Word for Windows, Excel for Windows.

The difference between Object Linking and Object Embedding is as follows:

1. Object Linking is when there is only one copy of the object. Applications that use the same object only really store a link to this object. If you edit or change the object, then all linked objects in other applications will be updated automatically.

2. Object Embedding is when you embed a copy of the object in another application. Editing the object will only change the copy that is in the application being used. Other copies of the object, which may exist in other applications, will not be affected.

A linked or embedded object may be accessed for editing from any of the applications using it. Just double-click on it and the application that created the object will be started automatically, with the object displayed, ready for editing. If the object is linked then all the links will be updated. If it is embedded then only the copy in the current application will be updated.

Another similar technique is DDE (Dynamic Data Exchange). This allows you to set up links between common data in different applications so that changes to data in one application will be reflected in others automatically. Unlike OLE, DDE requires all its applications using linked data to be open before you can make changes to the data.

Note
You can link and embed objects from another computer by first connecting to a ClipBook, selecting a shared page and copying it into your own Clipboard.

Linking an Object

Tip
Use Object Linking to automatically update an object in several documents.

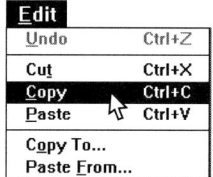

1. Start the application which has the object you want to link. In this example we will use Paintbrush. If you are not familiar with Painbrush, refer to Chapter 6.

Tip
If you have just created an object, save it before trying to link it into another application.

2. Create your object, or if it has already been created, choose **O**pen... from the **F**ile menu to load the file containing the object. e.g. a logo is loaded in the drawing area as shown.

3. Click on the Pick tool from the toolbox and drag the mouse from the top left corner outside the object to the bottom right corner. The object will then be boxed in a broken line.

4. Click on **C**opy from the **E**dit menu. This copies the object to the Windows clipboard.

5. Minimise or Close the Paintbrush window.

6. Start the application you want to link the object into. Here we are using Write (see Chapter 6 on how to use it).

7. Click on the Paste **L**ink option from the **E**dit menu in Write. This will link the object at the current insertion point.

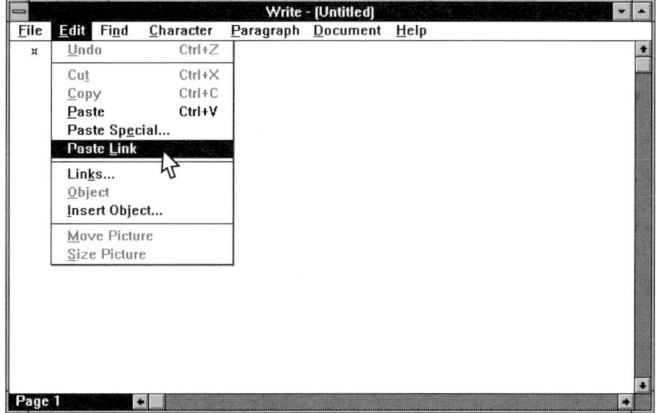

Tip
Select Links... to display information on linked objects. You can Cancel Link or choose Manual updating to control when the object gets updated.

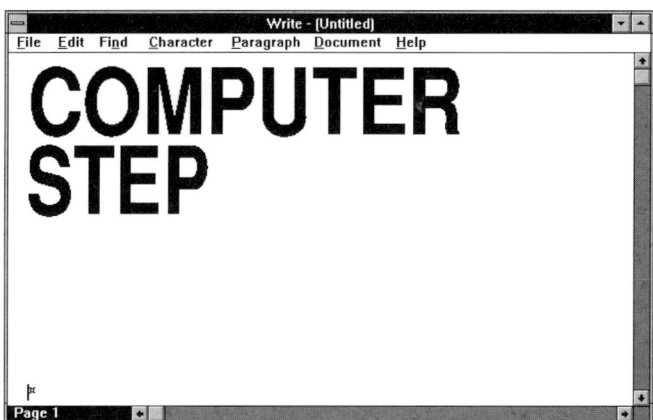

Embedding an Object

Embedding an Object is exactly the same as Linking it except, choose **P**aste instead of Paste **L**ink from the **E**dit menu.

Note
You can embed objects into Mail messages to send them to other users on your network.

Tip
Use Object Embedding to easily copy objects and then to manipulate them in different ways.

Changing a Linked Object

Tip
Click on the Object to select it. It'll be highlighted and you can Cut or Copy it from the Edit menu, or press the Del key to delete it.

Tip
Any change you make must be within the boundary of the object - otherwise it will not be reflected in applications the object is linked in.

1. Double-click on the linked object from any application that uses it (e.g. Write). The application that the object was originated from or the one that created it is then launched automatically (e.g. Paintbrush).

2. Edit the object as required and save the changes.

3. Access the original application or any other application that uses the linked object to see the changes that you have made.

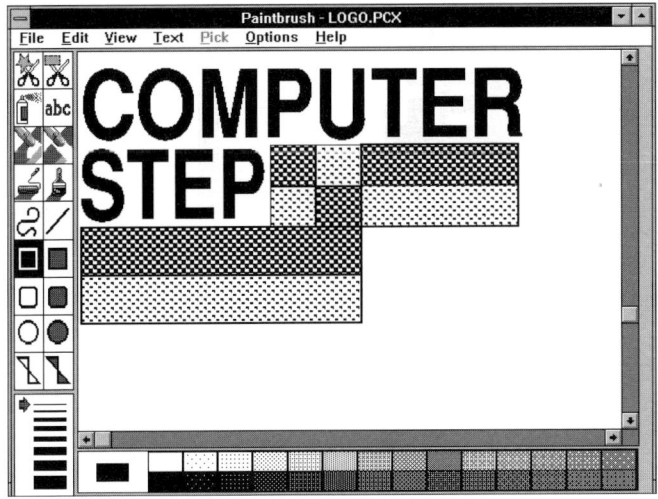

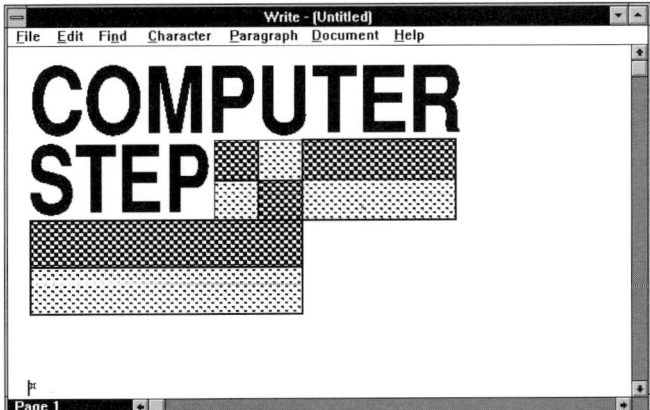

Note

If a logo, as in our example, was object linked into all documents requiring it (e.g. as part of a letterhead), then a change in the company logo may be reflected in all documents using it - instantaneously!

Changing an Embedded Object

Changing an embedded object is exactly the same as changing a linked object. The only difference is that only the object being edited is altered. Any other copies of the object that may exist will remain un-altered.

Using Object Packager

Object Packager

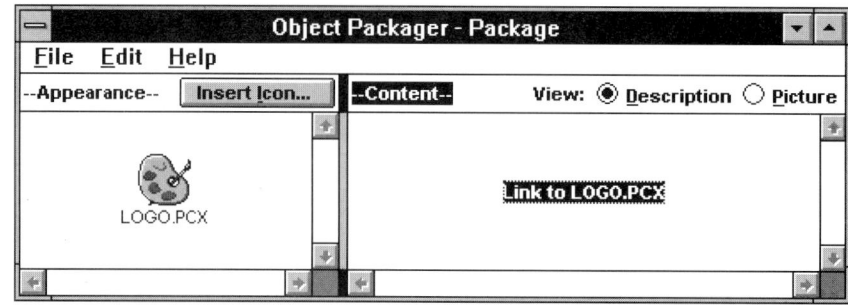

Note
Object Packager is part of the accessories group.

Object Packager is a tool used to insert a linked or an embedded object into a document. It represents an object as an icon. This icon is the default one for the application that created the object, but you can change it to an icon of your choice.

To place an object into the Object Packager, choose Import... from the File menu and import the file containing the object. You can change the icon by clicking on the Insert Icon... button. To view the object, just click on the Picture option. Then to insert the object in a document, choose Copy Package from the Edit menu. This copies the package to the clipboard. Finally, from the destination application, choose Paste.

Index

A

Anti-Virus 89
Application groups 9
Arranging icons 15
Automating startup 49

B

Backing up 90

C

C:\. *See* MS-DOS Prompt
Calculator 138
Calendar 137
Cardfile 136
Character Map 139
Chat 3, 142-143
Check boxes 10
Clipboard 41. *See also* ClipBook
ClipBook
  connecting to shared 47
  copying pages to Clipboard 45
  deleting pages 45
  disconnecting from shared 47
  displaying pages 44
  saving from Clipboard 42
  sharing pages 46
  unsharing pages 46
Clock 135

Control menu box 20
Control Panel 96, 111-123
Cursor blink rate 116

D

Date 119
DDE. *See* Dynamic Data Exchange
Desktop 9
  accessories 129-140, 180
  colours 111-112
  organising 50-52
  pattern 113
  wallpaper 114
Device contention 121
Dialog boxes 10
Directories
  changing 62
  connecting to shared 67-68
  copying 74-77
  creating 64
  current 55
  deleting 78
  disconnecting from shared 71
  expanding/collapsing branches 63
  moving 74-77
  parent 55
  renaming 81
  seeing shared use 69-70
  sharing 65

  undeleting 79
  unsharing 66
  viewing 57
Directory window 55
Disk
  copying 88
  formatting 86
  labelling 87
Disk drive icons 55
Disk drives 62
Drag and Drop printing 98-99
Dynamic Data Exchange 175

E

Enhanced Mode 121
EPS 95

F

Fast Alt+Tab switching 116
Fax Facilities 3, 148
File and Disk access 32-bit 121
File Manager 55-90
  customising the Toolbar 124-125
  Mail messages 158
Files
  associating with applications 84
  changing attributes 83
  copying 74-77
  deleting 78

document 55, 58
hidden 55, 58
moving 74-77
program 55, 58
renaming 81
searching for 82
selecting 72-73
sorting 59
starting application
  from 85
system 55, 58
undeleting 79-80
viewing 57-58
viewing information 58
Fonts 61, 132
  installing 96
  TrueType. *See*
    TrueType Fonts

G

Graphical User Interface
  1
Group icons 9
Group window
  cascading 17
  closing 20
  deleting 30
  moving between 16
  scrolling 19
  setting up 30
  sizing 14
  tiling 18

H

Help
  annotating 126
  bookmark 126
  using 21-23

I

Icons 1, 9-10
  rearranging 15
  spacing 116
International settings 120

K

Keyboard response 118

L

Logging off 147
Logging on 147

M

Mail 3, 151-164
  administrator
    151, 153
  creating new folders
    162
  deleting messages 161
  exiting 164
  folders 159
  message options 159
  moving messages
    between folders 163
  private folders 162
  reading messages 160-
    161
  replying to messages
    160-161
  sending messages 157-
    158
  shared folders 162
  signing in 156
Media Player 140
Menu 10

Menu bar 9
Microsoft Anti-Virus. *See*
  Anti-Virus
Microsoft At Work PC
  Fax. *See* Fax Facili-
  ties
Microsoft Backup. *See*
  Backing up
Modem 139
Mouse 7, 117
MS-DOS Prompt 48
Multimedia 121, 140
Multitasking 2, 38-40

N

NetWatcher 144
Network 2
  accessories 141-148
  card 3
  server 147
  settings 122
  setup 148
Notepad 135

O

Object Linking and
  Embedding 2, 175-
  179
Object Packager 180
OLE. *See* Object Linking
  and Embedding
Options 10

P

Paintbrush 133-134
Password 2
  logon 8, 147

Mail 165
Schedule+ 165
shared ClipBook pages 46
shared directories 65
shared printers 104
Path 55
PIF Editor 35-36, 48
Ports 121
Postoffice 3
   adding users 153
   changing user information 154
   removing a user 155
   setting up 151-152
Print Manager 100-108
Print screen key 41
Printers
   accessing 93
   connecting to network printers 106-107
   disconnecting from network printer 108
   installling 94
   pausing 101
   priority 102
   resuming 101
   setting up 95
   sharing 104
   unsharing 105
   using separator pages 103
Printing files 97-99
Program group
   setting up 29-30
Program items 9
   deleting 32
Program Manager 9
Programs
   setting up 31-32
   setting up several 33
   starting 37, 85
   switching 38-39
   working with several 38-40

R

Recorder 139
Remote Access 147

S

Save settings (on exit) 26
Schedule+ 3, 165-172
   adding appointments 166-167
   appointment book 166
   calendar 165
   exiting 172
   planner 171
   recurring appointments 168
   scheduling a meeting 167, 171-172
   signing in 165
   task list 169-170
Screen colours 111
Screen savers 115
Scroll bars 19
Sound 121
Sound Recorder 140
Startup group 49
Status bar 55

T

Task List 39-40
Terminal 139
Time 119
Title bar 9
Tree window 55
TrueType fonts 61, 132

V

Viruses
   scanning for 89
Volume label 55

W

WFWG. *See* Windows for Workgroups
Wildcard characters (?,*) 73, 82
Window
   border width 116
   closing 20
   directory 55
   frame 11
   granularity 116
   maximise button 12
   minimise button 13
   moving 11
   multiple 60
   restore button 12
   scrolling 19
   splitting 56
   tree 56
Windows for Workgroups 1
   exiting 25
   starting 8
WinMeter 144
WinPopup 145-146
Workgroup 2
Write 130-132

Other in easy steps Books

TITLE	AUTHOR	ISBN	PRICE
Windows 3.1	Harshad Kotecha	1-874029-02-4	£9.95
WordPerfect 6 for Windows	Kate Stewart	1-874029-11-3	£14.95
PageMaker 5 for Windows	Scott Basham	1-874029-06-7	£14.95
Word 6 for Windows	Scott Basham	1-874029-16-4	£14.95
Excel 5 for Windows	Roy Roach	1-874029-15-6	£14.95

"...beautifully clear and simple to follow. ....You WPWIN6 users can be sure you will bless the day you got it."

WordPerfect User Group

"...is quite the best book on this subject I have read. The use of concise explanations with copious pictures is the obvious way to learn to use DTP packages and the author uses this technique brilliantly."

The IBM PC User Group

"...one of the best PageMaker 5.0 reference books on the market."

Aldus Magazine

"...well written, concise and relevant, meeting our needs very closely."

NatWest Bank

Computer Step publishes other computer books and provides on-site computer courses/consultancy. For further details please call 0926 817999.